1996 Gen...

S0-AVR-463

1996 Gen

For Janie —
See P. 92!

Love Love
Edie
Christmas, 1996

T R A N S M O N T A N U S

R E D   L A R E D O   B O O T S

Published by New Star Books

Series editor: Terry Glavin

Other books in the Transmontanus series

Red Laredo Boots

Theresa Kishkan

TRANSMONTANUS / **NEW STAR BOOKS** VANCOUVER

In memory of Gayle Stelter

You loved the sage, the dry air,
the long road home through the Canyon ...

CONTENTS

Pioneer
Jacket

for Solveigh and Joe

WALKING WITH THE HARRISONS after a holiday brunch, we take the road to Sakinaw Lake, in groups. Those in front are in an animated discussion about books and ideas. Solveigh, Angelica, and I follow behind, commenting on this and that, feasting our eyes on the soft green moss that hangs from the bare maples, on the deep stands of fern on the south side of Sakinaw Lake Road, and on the hill of tall firs rising off the north side. Angelica and I watch for the shrew mole that was nearly startled to death by our dog, Lily, a day or two before. She'd brought it gently up out of the grass in her mouth, up from its solitary tunnelling in search of insects and worms, and it had rested on the tops of the winter grasses, trembling, its nose twitching uncontrollably. We examined it closely so that we could look it up later in the mammal book, and when we left it was still, cradling its tiny head with forefeet that looked like small shovels. And there it was, untouched, its pelt bedraggled with rain.

These woods are so familiar, with their stands of old trees, and streams running down off mountains to enter the soft lakes. I've camped in

FACING PAGE: *One of the boys 'who dove from the wharf into the lake, impossibly young ...' Circa 1960.*

woods like this all my life. I've camped alone, I've camped with this family I've made with my husband, and I've camped with an earlier family – my parents and three brothers in the long summer days before my brothers left (one restless, one angry, the last one reluctant). In those days we'd pack up our station wagon, tie a boat to the frame on the car roof, and head to the west coast of Vancouver Island or the Gulf Islands.

I loved Saltspring, with its farms of untidy sheep and tart apples, its creosoted logs holding docks of greying boards, and its beaches of oysters and grey fog. At St. Mary's Lake, my father would rise early and push out onto the water in his homemade boat. He loved to fish at dawn, alone, and I'd lie in my sleeping bag, the smell of the old canvas tent over me like an eiderdown, hearing his oars in their creaky locks, the rattle of his fishing rod on the boat's slatted floor. Falling back to sleep, I'd hear his return as though in a dream, the oars almost silenced by water, our dog whining a greeting from the shore. Rainy days were best for fishing and there were always lots of those. On those mornings, the blue walls of tent would be patchy with water and we'd be warned not to touch the sides. A few mosquitoes would hum at the screened windows. I'd lie among my brothers, queen of the peaked tent, until the smell of cornmeal-dusted fish, sizzling in bacon fat, wakened my hunger. I never missed the privacy that was so important at home except when dressing, and then I'd pull off my pyjamas within my sleeping bag and pull on my clothes, which would always be wet with condensation or rain – usually they hung on the ribs of the tent poles and I'd reach up, holding my pillow to my chest, and grab a shirt. It was almost impossible to button it properly in the confines of a sleeping bag, and it would stick to my skin unpleasantly. Going out to the wooden table I'd find a plate of buckwheat pancakes, crisp from cooking in oil, and curling fillets of small-mouthed bass draining on paper towels. When I was old enough to drink coffee I'd help myself from the blackened pot on a stone by the fire, pour the smoky coffee into an old yellow cup, drink it down to almost the last gritty drop, and then read the pattern of grounds on the cup's bottom – once a heart, and several times islands in the shape of Australia.

If I took myself out in the boat later, I could still smell my father, old tobacco and his Pioneer jacket glazed with rain, a little pool of blood on the wooden slats where the fish had lain, their bellies opened with my father's sharp Buck, viscera thrown for the eagles. Sometimes he glided in to the shore attended by one or two young eagles, mottled and eager, the adults apparently disdaining such behaviour but close enough to beat the younger ones back should a handful of intestines be flung their way.

In those years at St. Mary's Lake, my brothers and I slept side by side in identical sleeping bags, roasted marshmallows over a fire at dusk, and explored an old farmstead with moss-covered apple trees dropping their fruit to rot in the tall wild grass. Would they remember any of the camping trips with the same affection, I wonder? One brother fought with my father well into his twenties, one brother moved far away, one wants nothing of memory. They are not the boys who dove from the wharf into the lake, impossibly young, their voices calling across the water like the poetry of Job: *Come thus far, I said, and no further: here your proud waves shall break*, and *Have you ever in your life commanded the morning or sent the dawn to its post, telling it to grasp the earth by its very edges?* and *Hath the rain a father?*

Those years seem so long ago now, walking with my friend and my own daughter down a road into vistas so dear and familiar – the island with the pictographs, in sight now; the abandoned garden where another friend and I dug up clumps of forget-me-nots, irises, poppies, and daisies; the maple seedpods that we whirl into the air like boomerangs, as I did as a child, and will again. My husband walks ahead in my father's old Pioneer jacket, still smelling of tobacco though it's been years since he owned it, all of us meeting again at the shore where two men are pulling in their aluminum boat, soaked through their waterproofs, four cutthroat already gutted on the floor of the boat. Our friends look down the lake, seeing something of what everyone sees but newly and freshly, the air cleansed with rain. The quartet of fish is so beautiful, the dark speckled bodies slashed at the gills with brilliant red, and the smell of their blood is something I take all the way home, threaded on a small forked stick.

Crow's Nest in
the High Trees

I SWIM TWO MORNINGS a week in a local public pool during an allo-
cated hour called Ladies Swim. Sometimes there are two or three others in the pool, seldom four. I've never been a good swimmer but all
summer I plunge daily into the lake adjacent to my property with my
family and I roll and surge and float on the placid water, feeling buoy-
ant and purposeful in a way I seldom feel on land. I like the way the
knots of tension at the back of my neck unwind themselves as I stretch
my arms forward. So twice a week during fall and winter I go to the pool
to swim laps.

The chlorine bothers my eyes so I swim with my head above water,
the sidestroke usually. I move up and down my lane, thinking of chores,
books, thinking of a interior by Bonnard, *La préparation du dîner*, and
how the plates for the meal are really just a few casual lines against a
white cloth. A bottle of wine, some fruit, other implements, and a
woman to one side, bending over a task. This leads me to think of how
lovely Bonnard's dining room is with its Naples yellow walls and large
windows. I think of my own family's dinner, wondering what I ought to
make, should I defrost a chicken, have we enough wine, and so on. I

swim and think and often there is music, Eric Clapton or reggae on the pool's sound system, the guitar bouncing off the water and warbling a little. I don't have much time during the week when I am so free to think of nothing but what comes into my head. Usually there are the chores associated with running a household of five people, of gardens, laundry, my writing; and often I am thinking of just what needs to be done next, whether it's a sentence in a paragraph or a row of spinach to plant or bread dough that must be punched down for loaves as soon as I'm finished the dishes. It gives my life focus of course, and purpose, but at times I like just to move one arm ahead of the other, to glide through the water with an image in my head and the free association that follows.

Lately, during my swim, I've noticed a nest in the stand of evergreens outside the pool. It's a large one and messy so I think it must belong to a crow. There are certainly a lot of crows about. At the elementary school, just a few miles away, many of them wait on the chain-link fence for the children to come out with their lunch bags. They tussle over crusts and even whole sandwiches. They're noisy, always arguing and exclaiming, except when the eagles who patrol the high trees by the government wharf drift over the field. Then there is silence and stillness on the part of the crows unless they are protecting their young. Then they are brave beyond imagining.

I swim and watch the nest, hoping to see a crow alight on the bridge of branches that holds it. This would be a good place for a crow to raise young because the pool is located at the high school, near the soccer field, so lunch scraps would be readily available. The trees are high enough that no one would climb them to take eggs or poke at the nest with the end of a hockey stick. And a creek winds its way to Oyster Bay just to the south of the school, its banks littered with salmon bodies come autumn, pulled from the water by raccoons and bears. A grove of tall trees just to the west of the soccer field probably contains other nests because crows tend to gather in colonies. This one, in proximity and yet removed, may be the nest of a loner, perhaps the crow with one white flash on its left wing that I've seen on the field as I park my truck before my swim.

Swimming, I am at once energized and relaxed. Up and down, touch the pool edge and kick off again. Side stroke, back stroke, pushing through the water in a rather inept breast stroke that feels terrific, taking deep breaths and blowing out vigorously. On the first day of March I am swimming up and down thinking about gardening. I've begun to dig out my main vegetable beds and to lightly fork a barrow-load of compost into each. If I'm lucky, I'll be able to bring home a utility trailer of horse manure from a place just to the south of the pool – and a barrowful of the richly dark manure spread on the flower and vegetable beds, as well as several loads distributed around the fruit trees, is a great way to begin the gardening season. All around while I dig, the robins will be waiting to explore the newly turned soil where the fat earthworms tunnel their way to the surface. Once I found two worms entwined in the dark earth and I burst into tears at the beauty and mystery of it. I find their eggs sometimes, small and yellow like opaque planets.

I like the way the big windows beside the pool frame the trees so fully, arched over by a blue sky like a book of hours on the first of March. When I'm swimming from the shallow end to the deep, I can see the knob of Mount Daniel from certain angles. Swimming back, after kicking emphatically from the edge of the deep end, I look northwest towards my house. I love windows, the changing views, the way they make a kind of art of the day. In my house there are pictures that I cherish from many of the windows. I was reading in my living room one fall evening and I saw a bright light fall from the sky. It happened so quietly that I wasn't sure I'd seen it until I read in the local newspaper a day or two later that someone who knew about such things saw a meteorite falling. I realized then that was what I must have seen. Imagine casually looking up from your book (what would it have been – the stories of Chekhov, maybe?) to see a meteorite falling past your house while all around you people wash dishes, balance their chequebooks, sing.

In my study I look south to some mature arbutus, now in bud with the candelabra of creamy blossom that will smell so strongly in a month or so. The window is protected by a small overhang of second-storey sundeck, the underside of which is latticed with cedar and laced with wisteria. Once, last spring, I sat working at my desk and realized that something I'd dreamed of was right in front of my eyes: a haze of wisteria blossoms hanging from the lattice, lavender, framed with pale green leaves. It was so unexpectedly lovely that I recorded the moment in my journal. These days when I work at my desk, I look out and remember and hope for the same thing this year. Bonnard's studio in his little house at La Cannet looked out at some red-tiled roofs, sharp yucca, and a glorious mimosa tree. One of my favourite paintings is his *L'atelier au mimosa*, full of sun and light. The same tree might have provided the arrangement for *Bouquet de mimosas*, painted five or six years later, but the heavy branches, in a glass bowl, are not so fresh and yellow as the studio view has them. As beautiful as Bonnard's interiors are, the light-spangled bathrooms, the rich dining rooms with their red drapery, I always feel his palette comes to life outside, washed with the clear Mediterranean light. The view of La Cannet, caught from a hill just above his house, with the greens and soft russet rooftops; the garden steps through a blaze of mimosa; all the garden canvases but particularly *Le jardin* of 1937 with oleander, and one of the orange trees hanging with ripe fruit that gave his house its name, Le Bosquet.

In early April, a week after a strong windstorm, I am several laps into my swim before I notice that I can no longer see the nest in the tall tree. Thinking that the tree is just fuller in its spring growth, I side-stroke up and down the pool facing the windows so that I can see the tree from various angles. No, the nest is gone: blown down, no doubt, by the fierce gales that rocked my own house a few miles further up the coast. When I'm finished my swim I go out to the trees and look all around under the one where the nest was, to see if I can find a remnant of it to take home. There's a fair bit of wind-litter around, small branches, the new cone-bearing tips of fir trees, rust-coloured cedar fronds, but nothing that looks like a crow's nest. Perhaps the whole thing simply blew into a nothingness of twigs in a strong gust of wind, the crow nowhere to be seen in such weather. Or, like the house in *The Wizard of Oz*, the nest

The Tool Box

When the wind is southerly, I know a hawk from a handsaw.
— Shakespeare, *Hamlet* II.ii

1

MY HUSBAND JOHN was five years old and his sister was two years younger when their parents left England in 1953, two years before I was born. I think his parents were disappointed with England in those years of rationing and depression after the war. They were from Sheffield, a city that had received more than its share of bombs, and I think that they wanted a fresh start for themselves and their children. John's father had spent four years as a prisoner-of-war in Bavaria, a time of pain and trauma, but also, ironically, of opportunity – he'd completed a degree in economics from Oxford by correspondence, arranged by the Red Cross. John's mother had spent part of the war years working in the Land Army, billeting on farms where she'd milk cows and help with harvests, a time that she remembers happily. The farms weren't bombed, as was her

FACING PAGE: *Harold Pass at his workbench in Sheffield, England,* circa 1950.

Red Laredo Boots   17

house in Sheffield, which had received an incendiary device neatly through its roof; the bomb landed on her bed. She was with the rest of her family in the bombshelter at the time, home for a few days' respite from the farm work. The bomb burned the mattress and scorched an adjacent dresser until the *All Clear* sounded and the family came up to put the fire out. That dresser is in her guest-room in Nanaimo now, a small scar on its surface. When her fiance – for that was what he was to her then – returned from Germany after the war, I think they wanted a quiet productive life; they thought he would get a job, they'd buy a house and raise a family and spend holidays the way they both liked, hiking in Cornwall or the Lake District. For some years, though, they lived in a trailer, all that was available, and when they were finally able to buy a house, they realized that they'd been deeply soured by England. John's mother's brother, Uncle Eric, had trained as an RAF navigator in Canada in the early years of the war, and as soon as he was demobilized after the armistice, he took his new bride to Calgary. He wrote letters urging his sister and her young family to come to Canada. There were so many opportunities, open spaces, no rationing, and best of all, the Rockies were visible from their home in Calgary. My husband's family sold their house and packed up a few household effects to ship to Canada, including a wooden bedside lamp, curtains, and one or two special wedding gifts such as a silver coffee jug with an eagle on the lid. They took an ocean liner, the *Atlantic*, to Quebec City. From there they travelled by train to Calgary and began the rest of their lives.

Something else they brought with them, apart from the household effects, was a tool box my husband's grandfather had made as a farewell gift to his emigrating son. He was a cabinet maker, and I suppose he couldn't imagine anything more useful for beginning again in a new country than a box of tools. He made the tool box himself, dovetailing the pieces neatly together and outfitting the box in a careful, precise way. I can see him making lists of tools that he knew to be indispensable in his own life, checking his tool box to see what he didn't need or could give up. He wasn't wealthy, but he believed in quality – the tools were first-rate, the blades and bits and chisels all Sheffield steel. And this box rode the *Atlantic* to Canada, all those years ago.

2

MY HUSBAND AND I built our own house, a cedar-sided, shake-roofed frame house on a bluff facing southwest. From the upstairs bedroom you can see little flashes of Sakinaw Lake through the trees and to the east is Mount Hallowell, our own peculiar weatherglass: if we can see the peak, it's likely to be a fine day; if it's shrouded in mist, then we expect rain. The moon rises above one green shoulder, and in the fall we take note of the progress of snow making its way down the slope.

We knew nothing about house building, but we wanted to do it ourselves, partly because we knew it would be cheaper that way and partly because we thought it was important to have a house that reflected our own needs and hopes (windowsills for plants, windows facing south and west for good light, rooms for every purpose). We began the house when we had our first baby, camping on our worksite and setting him in a stroller to watch as we framed walls, nailed plywood, and strapped the roof. As it turned out, we had a larger family than we thought we would – three children instead of just one or maybe two. We found it difficult to share a workroom with each other, and we wanted a plant room when we began to make gardens in earnest, so we ended up adding two new parts to the original structure.

We bought tools as we needed them, nothing really fine or special, but a basic orange Black and Decker circular saw, a good hammer, nailsets, a plumb-bob, a level, chisels, a drill, and a square. We learned about building as we went along, asking questions and thinking about things carefully before actually doing them. The work went slowly but surely, and just before our second child was born we moved in to an unfinished but liveable house. We put mats over the plywood floors until we could afford to tile and carpet them and set a kitchen sink into a piece of ply-wood nailed to sawhorses until we could manage kitchen counters and cupboards. The spring after our third child was born, we built a wing with little rooms for small children. We discovered several years later that they really needed more space, so we added another two rooms on the ground floor, knocking out walls between the former little rooms to make a big one, and covering it all with a flat tarred roof which we built a sundeck over, glassing in part of it to make a sunroom. Now there are vines growing up all the walls – grape, clematis, rose, and trumpet. The shakes and siding have all weathered to a uniform colour and you can't tell which is the original house and where the new parts begin.

3

SOME YEARS AFTER we'd begun our house and acquired our own set of tools, John's mother offered us a battered wooden tool box that had been sitting in her basement. My husband remembered the box from his childhood as a place where you could find a chisel when you needed to pry open a paint can or locate a small hammer for the occasional pounding of nails to hang pictures. His father had not been much of a carpenter. There had been a room finished in a basement once in a house they'd lived in outside Vancouver – a matter of nailing up some panelling and mortaring bricks to the surface of cement blocks that already formed a roughed-in fireplace. Mostly his father worked, and in his leisure he read travel books and typed careful itineraries of trips the family would take to the Rockies each summer. The family had moved from Calgary to Charleswood, near Winnipeg, and then moved out west to the coast, settling in Coquitlam, when John was a teenager. His par-ents separated when he was seventeen, and his father went to live in a bachelor suite in a high-rise apartment building in Victoria where he still lives, thirty years later, surrounded by his stereo equipment. My father-in-law lives a carefully regimented life. He walks a set number of miles per day. He spends a determined amount of money each year on packaged vacations to exotic locations. He drives his car once a week for groceries. When he visits us, he figures out how much money he saves on food by staying with us and then spends that precise amount on presents for us. The presents are things he's asked us to suggest on the phone a week or two before he visits, and they are always exactly what we have recommended – a soccer ball, books, stamps, special dark coffee beans, a cupcake doll. In between his visits there is no communication. Once we sent a Christmas card but he was embarrassed and told us not to expect the same from him. He never asks us about our lives or our hopes, and yet he does come once a year, a pattern established after the birth of our first child; before that there hadn't been contact for years. When he visits, there's the sense that he talks to us like he talks to random strangers in his life – a booking agent for a cruise ship line or the woman who sells him his weekly loaf of bread. The children adore him, in part because he tells good stories and he'll play Trivial Pursuit again and again and again without complaining.

My mother-in-law moved to Wellington, north of Nanaimo, to take a teaching job. She retired there in a house overlooking the sea, surrounded by a lovely garden. Periodically, she makes a point of passing along to us things with some family value – chairs that had belonged to her mother, some silver, curtains that had travelled in a container from England (though not on that original ocean voyage, but some years later when her mother died in Suffolk and some of her things were brought to Canada). I don't think the tool box was given in this spirit of sentiment. I think it had been left with her when her husband had made a rather surreptitious departure for Victoria and a new life, and she eventually wondered what to do with it. She had a few necessary tools of her own, and had no use for a heavy black box of broken hacksaws and old tobacco tins full of God knows what. We brought the box home and gave it a fairly cursory inspection, finding a place for it under the workbench in my husband's little workshop, and then more or less forgot it.

4

MY OLDEST SON loves family history. He's spent quite a lot of time mapping out both sides of our families as best he can on an enormous piece of graph paper, gathering photographs, certificates, and anecdotes. He has tape-recorded conversations with his grandparents, finding out things that I never knew, my husband never knew. The story about the incendiary bomb, for instance. I think my husband had heard something of that in his childhood but not with the vivid detail accompanying the story told to our son. And I never knew that my paternal grandmother had once held land speculators at gunpoint in Aberdeen, Washington, after she found out that some land they'd sold her was useless. I don't know what kind of gun, or even if it was loaded, but I do know that she got her money back.

My father-in-law helped my son with the names and dates of his family. Harold Pass was his father, an avid cyclist and a gardener who built a small greenhouse with an aviary attached, in which he kept linnets and canaries. A tree grew out of the middle of the greenhouse and was surrounded by a seat. He grew tomatoes and loved roses. He once won a job during hard times in Sheffield by turning up for the interview in his work-clothes with a box of tools. This was the man who made the black tool box.

We took the tool box out one stormy Sunday to look at it, setting it on the mat in front of the woodstove, and the first thing I noticed about it were the initials riveted to its top: *BP*, in brass. "Those are my initials," said my middle child, Brendan, touching them with a curious finger. "Mine, and Grandpa's, too."

The box had not been cared for. It was gouged, chipped, and dirty, with a leather handle cracked and dry with age. It was quite large – twenty inches long, seven inches wide, thirteen and a half inches high – and it wasn't until we opened it that I realized it was probably made of oak. I wonder if Harold Pass had made it of scraps that he had left over from some fine project. He obviously thought it would be more durable or practical painted black, for the exterior had been painted, a few stray brushstrokes marking the edges where the lid closes. Inside, it had been given a cursory brush of stain, the grain of the oak marked and nicked by tools. But a drawer, the length of the tool box but just four inches wide, made to fit inside, notched and dovetailed, had been polished and varnished to show the grain. Two little drawer-pulls, finely turned, are fitted elegantly on the front. Looking carefully at the drawer, I recognized it as rosewood, a wood used frequently in cabinet making for its beauty and fragrance. My husband has a lovely rosewood lapdesk, given to him by his mother and originally belonging to her father. It's been well kept and polished, and it does have a distinct odour, but this drawer smelled merely old and musty.

5

AN INVENTORY OF THE BLACK TOOL BOX

i. THE ROSEWOOD DRAWER, when opened, revealed: an assortment of hacksaw blades; a pot hook made by the blacksmith at Barkerville and given to me because I'd hung on the fence for an hour or so watching him at work (how it found its way to the tool box I don't know); a soldering iron, wooden-handled with a hefty tip which would be held in a fire to heat it; some files (one is certainly from the collection originally – a wooden-handled flat file – and then two more which have been added over the years, these being round files to sharpen chain saw blades; two of the files have the same turned handles as the soldering iron, the wood chipped and blackened by sweat).

ii. Against the inside back of the tool box, Harold Pass made a little rack to hold two things: a hacksaw, marked ECLIPSE, with a logo consisting of two overlapping circles with a bold E inside one of them, and MADE IN ENGLAND stamped proudly to one side; a six-inch-long spirit level made of light oak, beautifully smooth, with a brass face fitted on with four tiny brass screws. The part of the rack that holds the level has been carefully fitted with green felt to protect the surface of the level. There is no maker's mark on the level, so I wonder if it was made especially for the tool box. When it sits on my desk, I am delighted to see that it reads perfectly level.

iii. On one inside end of the tool box, a little bracket has been made to fit a small try square. The square that is in the box is not the one that came with it and that's why it doesn't fit. It has a beautiful beam, of dark burnished wood that a woodworking friend says is another kind of rose-wood, almost black with patina, with three diamond-shaped inlaid pieces of brass around the three brass rivets holding the blade to the beam. My husband said that it had come from his maternal grandfather, the one who had left him the rosewood writing desk. He reminds me that we use the try square that came with the tool box in our printshop, so I go out to get it. It has a four-inch mitred beam holding a seven-inch blade. The beam is steel with a bumpy surface and the words MADE IN SHEFFIELD ENGLAND stamped dead-centre. The bumpy surface feels very pleasing to a thumb. It fits the bracket perfectly.

iv. On the opposite inside end of the tool box is a single small holder, fitted on an angle – the sort of thing a door bolt might slide into. Nothing presently in the tool box fits it but *something* must have, because this box has been put together too carefully and thoughtfully for there to be a random fitting.

v. On the inside of the lid of the box, there's a bracket which my husband remembers once held a handsaw. Using a saw of ours, he shows me how the bracket held the handle of the saw firmly in place and how the end of the blade fitted neatly into a little slot at the other end, now split and broken.

vi. In the box itself, not in any particular order: a hand-drill, with STANLEY, ENGLAND stamped on it; a small wooden box of bits, some of them unlike anything I've ever seen; three chisels, their handles broken and smeared with paint, their blades chipped and paint-smeared too (two of the chisels are the mortise type and one is a paring chisel – all three with worn illegible printing stamped into the tarnished blades); a folding metal rule stamped FOREIGN; a handmade tin box with five compartments in the bottom for holding screws and soft wooden plugs to be driven into walls to hold pictures, and a removable box fitting in on top with five compartments holding finishing nails; the head of a ball-peen hammer stamped HARDY PICK LTD. SHEFFIELD ENGLAND; a delicate finishing hammer stamped with something illegible and then SHEFFIELD; a woodworking screwdriver; a whetstone set into a handmade box of mahogany, elegantly bevelled, the marks of the chisel evident inside the lid. There are also two small tin tobacco boxes, ST. BRUNO FLAKE, which still hold grease. I've no idea what *kinds* of grease – one type is an opaque brown and the other a glossy reddish-brown. Both smell pleasant, but not like any particular grease, not, for instance, like the oil my father used for his whetstone, a delicious smelling oil that scented the whole basement when he was sharpening his hunting knives. I remember sitting on the basement stairs, listening to the blades being ground across the stone, and breathing in the heady oil.

6

WHEN WE'VE FINISHED looking into the tool box, we talk a little about a brief summer trip my husband's family made to England when he was a young teenager. They visited both sets of grandparents. My husband remembers a quiet man with a soft cardigan in a row house in Sheffield and he remembers a greenhouse with a tree growing up through the middle. He doesn't remember the tool box being referred to and doesn't remember it as being anything special when he was growing up. There were many trips in later years, but by that time Harold Pass had died.

A few weeks after my family looked at the tool box, I get it out and spread the tools around in my workroom to get a sense of it all again – the careful fittings, the thoughtful selection, even down to the little tins of grease. Did Harold Pass not know that there would be grease to oil and protect tools in Canada? Where did he think his son was going? Perhaps it seemed like the end of the earth to this man, a quiet carpenter who loved birds and growing things, and who obviously believed in taking care of his tools and using the right implement for the job. The family objects that have come from my husband's mother all arrived with their stories and the sense that they must be cared for. When my mother-in-law visits, she often offers to polish the oak chairs that were *her* mother's, wanting us to honour them in ways that we are reluctant to accept. But this box came to us with almost nothing, no story, no history except what my husband could remember. And after looking at the tools and the way they have been chosen and given a place, I find I feel growing affection for this man I never met or even thought about before. His own son must have seemed a puzzle to him, with his wanderlust and gift for languages, with his loud personality and unconnectedness to home and family. My husband remembers that a letter would be written to his grandfather once a year from Canada, a cursory account of the year. And no one even remembers the year that Harold Pass died, though there must be a certificate somewhere, or a note in a diary, or something. I wish there was a way to let him know that I'm sorry his gift was neglected for so long and that it has ended up so shabby and incomplete, missing its saw and ham-mer handle. I'd like to tell him that I mean to clean up the tool box – I don't know if I will, but I mean to, and that's a beginning (I have the per-fect stuff, a lavender-scented beeswax that I bought in a museum shop, thinking to treat the oak chairs to some proper care). I'd like to have asked him how the different woods felt when he was working with them, if he preferred the rosewood with its fragrance and grain, and if it was difficult to get the little level to read so perfectly. I'd like to tell him of his grandson's love of house building, and of a great-grandson, quiet and cir-cumspect, bearing those special initials. I'd like to tell him he would be remembered for his linnets and his greenhouse on a boy's family chart, half a century and a continent away.

Morning Glory

I'D NEVER NOTICED the way the fences of bleak houses lining the freeway out of Burnaby and Surrey were draped with morning glory, green leaves and the white trumpets covering chain-link and boards indiscriminately. Some of the houses had gardens but many had nothing but morning glory – it was mid-morning as we drove out – and I remembered a house I'd lived in as child, for a few months only, until something better came along. The house made my mother cry. I didn't know why then but I do now, remembering the paint flaking away from the board siding, the kernels of mice shit in the closets and cupboards, and the remnants of peonies and roses overgrown with morning glory. I thought it was beautiful, having little knowledge of gardens in those days, and I thought my mother wept unnecessarily and for too long. These houses brought it back and I could imagine the smell of the morning glory, sweet and rampant, bees deep in the white throats. I thought it meant something and wrote into my notebook "Morning glory" and the date, July 10, 1989.

We were going northeast, to the Nicola Valley, a place of deep visceral sensation for me. Once over the summit of the Coquihalla Highway, past the signs indicating stops for the old Kettle Valley Railway – Iago, Romeo, Desdemona ... who named these rocks and cliffs and from what unlikely perspective? – the land changed suddenly. High mountains and little leaps of snow and the larger glaciers gave way to the pines and pungent grey-leaved plants of the interior: artemisias and mulleins were those I knew. Bent forms of sagebrush and the pigment of earth made me want to cry, though not in the manner of my mother; I felt I was home.

We headed toward Nicola Lake, to Monck Park, named for a rancher's son who had been killed in World War II. The children, at this point, would have had their fingers crossed in hopes of a good campsite. I found myself wondering if the son had played in those hills and woods as a boy, thinking, What a heaven for a child – the red soil and hawks, the volcanic slope riddled with burrows, ospreys on the thermal drafts, and down on the lakeshore, the remnants of kikuli pits where the Indians had wintered, using the cliff face above Nicola Lake as their compass.

Just before the park, the little town of Nicola. The house where the rancher's family had lived was the most beautiful of all – a tall white Victorian structure with a turret, and the morning sun carved into the fretwork at the peak of the gable. The yard was surrounded by a picket fence nearly hidden by old lilacs. A small church with a graveyard: this would be visited later. When I closed my eyes, I could smell the newly cut hay as we drove the last bit of road, and the children remembered each landmark with excitement: marsh and apiary, wooden sign, last summer's trail.

We all agreed we'd found the best campsite. A few good pines scattering their large cones for our fire and a view of Quilchena across the lake. And the smell of sage and strong herbs everywhere. We tucked little clumps of lad's love and yarrow into our sleeping bags. Did the boy play here where my children slept, did he climb where we climbed to collect lava? In those days did the Indians still winter on the shores of Nicola Lake or had they already retreated to their reserve? Would the boy have passed them as he rode with the men to bring the cattle down off their summer range?

My children dug in the sand and caught minnows and rolled down the soft grass into the kikuli pits. They brought plants for me to identify and then left them to dry on rocks, their fingers stained with the bitter oils. In the mornings I closed my eyes and heard nothing but the gutteral *kraaa* of the nutcrackers and the chittering of the squirrels and chipmunks. *Anyone ever here would have heard this.*

Why did I feel such longing and feel it now, remembering? I may have passed through this country as a child but have never lived here, have no deep knowledge of its plants and sky. Yet each breath of air was like memory.

The hills across the lake were like the flanks of horses, rippling as the clouds passed over. The same clouds were caught in the bowl of lake and I watched my oldest son swim through the shadows, his body moving in the dark water then rising out to climb the wooden raft. There was wind and the clouds passed and he swam back in sunlight. It wasn't fear I felt as he swam in the shadowy water but the knowledge of loss. It hung in the air.

On trips to Nicola in the past I'd visited the graveyard and the little church, relics both of a time before the boy's death. In the graveyard were little cacti and irises gone wild and the grey herbs. Mothers and daughters buried together under rough stones in the unbearable stillness of grass. A young boy's stone in a wrought-iron enclosure, covered over by wild clematis. No stone for the rancher's son though the father had one: "Still achieving, still pursuing, with a heart for any fate." I went from grave to grave recording names and dates, as if that would tell me the nature of my place there. The dates shimmer in my notebook now as I puzzle over them, knowing that when these dead were laid in the ground my own grandparents were children in Eastern Europe and that my dead lie under stones a thousand miles away, in Alberta's badlands, though in a similar ground – no pines and resiny smoke but sparse grey plants and the incense of their own sad liturgy. And what I half-expected to find in the graveyard, I found: morning glory; but a smaller pink form, the field bindweed, strewn among the rusting rails of a beloved mother.

In the distance, a lone horse and rider. I wrote that down. At each turn in the road, my heart strained like a bird. It was as if. As if.

After lunch at the old hotel, the children played under poplars, not seeing the nest and feathered wedge of a tail poking out. Their father, lying in the cool grass, showed them. My middle child climbed a low hill and I watched him disappear from sight, but still heard him sing "On the Wings of a Dove" as he dreamed on the hill's far side. The red wine loosened my heart a little, enough to enter the stone store and try on an oilskin that a rancher might wear, buy the strong honey from the fields we passed on our way to the campsite. The boy might have ridden there with a list: tea, flour, something for the horses. This would have been the telegraph office. (Did the message come here from Europe, telling of his death? Grief figures in the lilacs about the house, has something to do with the bare windows of the turret – did he sleep there? – the unused look of the porch where the sun still radiated in the old dry wood of the gable.) Across the lake, the cliff above our campsite shone like the north star.

Each breath of air like memory ...

I filled my lungs with the resiny pine smoke and held it in to cloud my brain and heart. Walking the dog at night, I felt the land in each foot-step. *Touch the gaillardias, pale asters. Hand to the rough bark of the pine trees. Wind in the poplars rustling softly. Ospreys at rest in their twiggy eyries. Breathe in and remember.*

My children had their questions, who lived there and when, are there rattlesnakes and why not, who is God. I imagined the boy watching them from a far place, the rubble of the volcano, maybe, as they climbed the sign with his name on it. He would have known about the blackbirds weaving their nests like baskets and fastening them to strong reeds in the marsh before the lake. Would he have found the ossified droppings of marmots on the lava face and imagined them valuable?

When the naturalist told us that the droppings had often fooled early prospectors, who thought they were deposits of rare minerals, my sons found it terribly funny and hoped to find some to bring home. But all we found was bear scat on the trail by our campsite and a dead squirrel in the golden grass. Watching the shadows of clouds climbing down the hills and entering the lake, I had an answer for God but couldn't find my children to tell them.

When we got ready to leave the valley, I tried to work out directions for the quickest route away. I didn't think I could bear the slow way out, the one winding north of Quilchena and passing the ranches, the sweet grassy hills. Unpacking my suitcase a week later, I could smell pine-smoke in my sweater. There were seeds of wild grass in my socks, and the hooked memory of thistles.

In my notebook, "Morning glory" and the date, July 10, 1989. In later gardens, my mother planted a cultivar of morning glory called Heavenly Blue, perhaps forgetting what the white form had done to the roses and peonies. The blues were annual and I don't remember if they were invasive. Seeds of wild flowers come in the droppings of birds and mammals, hair and fur, the clothing of those passing through. In one corner of the graveyard at Nicola, a tendril of pink field bindweed among the small stinging cacti. In an enclosure of white pickets, a woman who died in childbirth and the daughter who survived her for nineteen days, dying on her mother's birthday, October 31, 1881, wild iris spreading over their little field of sadness. A young boy nearby, sleeping under the gentle cover of traveller's joy. God speed them all.

A Single
Starting Point

THE JUNCTION OF THE Yellowhead Highway 16 with the Cassiar Highway 37 is forty-three kilometres west of New Hazelton and ninety-one kilometres east of Terrace; you turn at the Skeena River bridge. *The Milepost* (1991) says that "kilometreposts are up along the Cassiar Highway about every 5 to 10 kms, but the posts do not accurately reflect driving distance nor are they measured from a single starting point."

LATE FEBRUARY, 1993

SOMETIMES WE HEAR a name and it rings in our heads like a tuning fork, playing each bone and sinew in a complex melody until we know it as part of ourselves, an attachment or mantra, I don't know which. And I don't know where I first heard *Telegraph Creek*, but suddenly I was aware of thinking it daily, imagining a place to go with the name, weathered wood and trails leading down to the river, the Stikine, thin dogs asleep on sagging porches and the smell of woodsmoke pinching my nostrils fiercely in cold air. I almost missed the brief newspaper piece on Telegraph Creek with a description of riverboat trips down the

FACING PAGE: *'Sometimes I think I was never meant to go there, having imagined the place so vividly already, messages coming across time and latitude ... ' Early Telegraph Creek.*

Stikine to Wrangell. A cafe was mentioned, a place where expeditions could be booked, and I thought to myself, well, one day I'll phone and see how it's done. And then I promptly forgot the name of the cafe, not even clipping the article to file under *Dreams*.

My husband, reading one of the books given him for Christmas, looked up to say, "The Stikine sounds like a fascinating river."

MID-APRIL, 1993

READING THE NEW *Harper's*, I was startled to see the words on the page, " … the old men of Telegraph Creek, a frontier hamlet on the Stikine River eight hundred miles north of Vancouver, British Columbia." The words belong to Edward Hoagland, a writer I have been peripherally aware of, having read essays here and there (in *Harper's*, in fact), but although I'd seen reference made to his book, *Notes From the Century Before*, I had no idea it was *about* Telegraph Creek. This essay was about something else entirely, but he was referring to how he used travel in his writing and I guess the most remote example he could cite was Telegraph Creek. The next time I met my husband for lunch at the college where he teaches, I took a few minutes to look up the book on the microfiche and order it from the college's main library (this is a small satellite campus in Sechelt). It arrived a week later and I read it nearly non-stop, irritated by the narrator almost beyond endurance (there's a dreadful part about being aroused by the bodies of dead deer, and his attitude toward the wives of the guides and a girl in Smithers is awful), but entranced by the country he wrote about. I talked to friends about the book and the country. My friend Charles Lillard, who grew up in Alaska, said, "Well, of course, everyone in the north wanted to shoot Hoagland after that book came out. They said he stayed about two weeks and told stories that were untrue and insulted just about everyone." But then my friend told me that he'd explored the area, too, and when I looked at a book of his, I realized that he'd even written poems about places like Meziadin and Dease Lake and yes, Telegraph Creek. I'd read these poems, of course, years before, and many times; why hadn't I remembered the place-names? I can only suppose that they'd remained silent beyond the page, hidden away until I was ready to hear them. Another friend said that one of the guides extensively quoted in *Notes from the Century Before* had told him that Hoagland had a severe speech impediment, alluded to in the book, and that people thought he was speaking a foreign language; he couldn't think how Hoagland imagined he'd had the conversations he reported so thoroughly in the book because people simply couldn't communicate with him.

What do I know about Telegraph Creek? Almost nothing. I do know that there was an attempt to link North America with the rest of the world by telegraph cable in the 1860s, the plan being to run cable from San Francisco through British Columbia and Alaska, then over the Bering Sea to Siberia to connect with existing cable through Russia to Europe. I think Telegraph Creek was to be a relay station in that fantastic plan, the place where the cable would cross the Stikine River on the route north. Supplies were brought upriver from Wrangell by paddle-wheeler to facilitate the erection of poles, housing for the crew, and so on. But the previously unsuccessful attempt to lay a submerged cable across the Atlantic finally worked and made the telegraph trail, already completed as far as the Kispiox River, unnecessary. I wonder about freezing and the almost impossible job of maintaining the lines through the most remote and unpopulated part of British Columbia. Natives used abandoned wire and insulators to build a suspension bridge across the Bulkley River and I've seen a photograph of it strung across Hagwilget Canyon, humming with its own strange messages.

And I know that there was a Hudson's Bay post in Telegraph Creek and that the building still stands, now the home of the cafe whose name I so promptly forgot. In *The Milepost*, there's a photograph of the building, its plain lines telling of hand-hewn timber. I can smell the shavings as the wood is planed to size, a little flutter of them drifting away in the wind.

The road in is difficult. *The Milepost* tells of "steep narrow sections and several sets of steep switchbacks." And it has its own weather. The road runs through lava beds, which sound fascinating, and there are Tahltan smokehouses where one can purchase smoked salmon. I hope there'll be somewhere good to camp. I imagine us on a river bar, a small fire, a box of food on the tailgate of the truck, scraping a frying pan in the cold water of the Stikine, scrubbing with sand. A pot of bitter coffee heating on a smooth riverstone set near the fire. I know nothing about the Tahltans (except that their bear-hunting dogs, now thought to be extinct, are commemorated on stamps), but I see their language, their names, on the map – Tahltan itself, a river running into the Stikine from the north, Casca on the ridge above Telegraph Creek, Spatsizi, meaning "red goat" from the habit of the mountain goats who roll in the ochre dust and who wander, thus marked, into their days.

May 28, 1993

AN ITEM ON THE NEWS reported that a man had successfully challenged a conviction of illegal hunting on the grounds that he had been charged with the offense but his five Native hunting companions hadn't been, and that the charge was a case of discrimination. The man and his friends had hired a helicopter out of Telegraph Creek to take them bighorn sheep hunting and apparently it's illegal to hunt from helicopters. I imagined them waiting on a flat plateau above the river for the helicopter to collect them, early morning mist rising from the water, their gear gathered in a heap. One has coffee in a thermos, maybe, and they sip and listen. They hear nothing but ravens and the idling of a truck warming up for the long drive to Dease Lake. I could see this so clearly that I was surprised to discover that I was still on my own sundeck, listening to the rest of the news while I drank a cup of coffee. I could smell the river from its great distance, cold and flinty, shaped by grizzlies as they fish for the rosy bodies of sockeye, come autumn, the currents meeting the huge bears and swirling around them in a watery deference.

December 21, 1993

I'D FORGOTTEN ABOUT Telegraph Creek these months after an aborted attempt to go there this past summer. We got as far as the Yellowhead Highway, planning to take the Cassiar Highway up to the Stikine. We'd been camping in rain for about a week, a few days in the Nicola Valley, sitting outside our tent under tarps, watching more rain clouds move in over the hills while gusts of strong wind blew our tarps and put our small fire out. We moved on to my brother's place in the Nazko Valley, sitting under tarps again while the kids donned raingear and fished for kokanee in my brother's lake. We grilled a kokanee over the open fire, the flesh sweet and smoky. Then we drove to Vanderhoof over the Blackwater Road, threading through wild country once crossed by Alexander Mackenzie on his trek from Lake Athabasca to Bella Coola. We stopped where he'd camped at Batnuni Crossing, the Native trading route, oolichan grease trails still visible under fine grasses and Indian paintbrush.

Our trip was not much of a success. The rain was constant, the mosquitoes worse; kids bickered in the backseat of the truck and our patience was strained. The town of Fraser Lake, which had a little of the magic of places that have watched significant history enacted on their soil, would have been beautiful in sunlight. We drove in late, pitched our tent in cold rain, sent the kids off for firewood, and tried to cook a dinner in clumsy raingear. Then we walked the dog, looking at other campers sitting under tarps. We saw entire campsites taken up by Winnebagos, television aerials perched on the top like huge dragonflies and the smell of something wonderful coming through the screens as the generators buzzed. We had the only sunny weather of our trip at Hazelton, a few brilliant days where we explored the several Hazeltons and 'Ksan. We wandered the riverfront, wrote postcards with cryptic messages to disguise the fact that no one was enjoying the camping trip thus far. We stopped at Hagwilget Canyon, with its fine bridge, and I stood there with my eyes closed, imagining the earlier bridge, ramshackle but anticipating this one with its location and purpose. We weighed and pondered the Cassiar Highway and had our minds made up for us by a convoy of mud-covered trucks we caught up to on the Yellowhead as we drove from our campsite into Hazelton to do our laundry.

"I bet they've just come off the Cassiar. Let's follow them and see if they stop so that we can talk to them."

We followed them into the lot of the Tourist Centre and waited while they got out and stretched a bit. Then I rolled down my window.

"Excuse me, did you just come down the Cassiar Highway?"

A man walked toward us, grinning. "How can you tell?" he asked.

"I think it was the mud. We were told that there are some unpaved stretches of the highway. Anyway, what kind of shape is it in?"

The man told us that their group of three trucks had come together from Alaska and that between them they had a broken axle, a cracked manifold, and a number of flat tires. He said that there were vehicles along the route pulled off with various broken parts waiting for tow-trucks to come from Dease Lake or Terrace. He blamed the weather, saying that the unpaved parts of the highway were mudholes and that we could probably get to Dease Lake unscathed if we went really slowly. The prospect of driving a washed-out road slowly with a cab full of rest-less children and a wet dog lying on the plywood floor of the canopy where some of us would be sleeping each night just seemed too awful to contemplate. I had somehow imagined us driving an excellent highway through virgin wilderness, grizzlies pausing politely at the roadsides to be photographed, the glaciers spectacular in the background. We decided we'd forego the drive up to Telegraph Creek at that particular time and go on to Prince Rupert instead. We spent another day at Hazelton, planning a side-trip to Kispiox to see the poles there.

We drove into the Kispiox Valley over hot roads and one-lane bridges, passing dusty aspens and a few startled grouse. After 'Ksan we expected something similar, with reconstructed longhouses, lawns with viewing areas of the Skeena, a shop selling modern frog bowls, beautiful and costly, and ponytail fasteners of rawhide. The guidebook told of the

'Ksan carvers and yes, their poles were splendid, paint fading already, but larger than life, numinous. What we hadn't known about 'Ksan was that you couldn't enter the carving house unless you paid for a tour. You couldn't enter any of the communal houses either, just the museum with its wonderful button blankets and shaman masks, and the giftshop. Groups were arranging themselves for the tour but I didn't want to be marched into the locked buildings, held at a distance, focussing a camera on the Eagles, the ever present Frogs, the Fireweed clan's Mosquitoes, or some crouching Wolves. So we drove to Kispiox late in the afternoon, hot and cranky.

We couldn't find the poles at first; there were no signs directing us to them. We followed our ears to the sound of the river, the Kispiox racing to meet the Skeena in a swirl of water, the gravel bars perfect for fishing. And that's where the poles were, fifteen of them in a little grassy field, overlooking the river, no information kiosk or brochure. They were magnificent, potent and alive in the sultry air. We lay in the hot grass, looking up at them – the One-Horned Mountain Goat, the Weeping Woman clutching her grouse, a sun-collared grizzly bear. Then we walked down to the river. Children were swimming off a gravel bar below a bridge, shrieking as they entered the cold water. I saw a car stop by the bridge and a number of children rush out to scramble down the bank to join those already in the water. I thought: they will have known this river all their lives, lived in anticipation of days like this when they can plunge in and splash, drifting on currents and tumbled by fast eddies, coming out to lie on the hot sand. We drove slowly back through Kispiox, seeing smoke billowing out of a smokehouse and dust rising off the road to meet it.

FEBRUARY, 1994

IT'S BEEN A YEAR since I first started thinking about Telegraph Creek, a single starting point in what became a journey of disappointments but one punctuated with small illuminations. Sometimes I think

I was never meant to go there, having imagined the place so vividly already, messages coming across time and latitude, however incorrectly I might have seen it in my mind's active eye. And I hadn't realized the distances involved in travelling there, or if I had, I'd somehow believed them to be familiar – the drive to Nicola or even the Rockies. When I spread out my maps to look at place names, they now sound with a harsh and inscrutable music: Meziadin, Iskut, Kinaskan Lake. In the photographs I've looked at, the Bear Glacier is blue and terrifying, yet on the map there's a figure of a skier deftly making his way down it. I see the Cassiar Highway littered with the bodies of broken-down cars and trucks, warnings to those who anticipated an easy drive all the way to Dease Lake or Upper Liard in the Yukon where the road meets the Alaska Highway. And yet one day, braver, more prepared, I hope we can join the convoy of dusty trucks making their slow way through a wild country threaded with rivers – the Stikine, the Nass, and that river of mists, the Skeena, tumbling from its headwaters just south of the Spatsizi Plateau where mountain goats climb on their sure feet, dirty white, or raddled like pictographs in the high mountain air.

Red Laredo
Boots

WE'RE HEADING TO THE INTERIOR for a few days away from the coast. We've all got the midwinter blues, long nights, short days, too much of this and that, housework, homework, bus rides for the kids that leave before it's light nearly and then a return ride at twilight. This ferry is the commuter one, not the locally nicknamed "Blood Vessel" which leaves at 6:30 a.m. and which is characterized by the sound of electric razors buzzing in the men's washroom, but the 8:30, freshly made-up women in business suits and other professionals heading to Vancouver for the day. I've spent some time looking among the bookshelves in the ferry giftshop for the ideal travel book for a family wanting to find history in weird and wonderful places, but everything seems too theme-driven: *Bed and Breakfast Hideaways, Hiking Trails in Southwestern BC, BC for Free.* I've forgotten to pack one or two favourites – *Historic Fraser and Thompson River Canyons, Merritt and the Nicola Valley* – but we have our maps showing the side roads and parks.

OUR DAUGHTER HAS BEEN studying Chinese New Year at school and it seems a good idea to walk the busy streets of Chinatown to give us all a sense of the exotic. Our own community has almost no ethnic diversity and the grocery stores have only a small section with tinned bamboo shoots and bags of dried chow mein noodles to give a festive touch at Chinese New Year. But the sidewalks on Pender Street and Main are filled with bins of bright vegetables and fruits, and shop windows are hung with glossy carcasses, wizened sausages, baskets of dried clusters that might be mushrooms or bear gallbladders. Roots of ginseng are something we recognize, and the familiar blue carp bowls of our own kitchen.

At Ming's we are shown to a table off to the side of a busy room. Women keep pushing the carts of dim sum to our table and we point to dishes of sticky rice, spring rolls, squid in ginger sauce, eggplant slices slit along one edge and stuffed with a single huge prawn then deep-fried, various dumplings with shrimp and pork, and we are given a large pot of tea. The children are conservative and only want the things they recognize, except the oldest boy who tucks into squid gladly, wondering aloud what this wonderful fish is, is told, turns green. John and I eat far more than we need, telling each other that we do this so seldom, a war of wills at work over the last eggplant slice.

Fueled for the journey, we finish our errands and head out the Trans-Canada Highway towards Hope. We plan to stop at the Tourist Information Centre in Chilliwack to find out about road conditions. Last week there was a blizzard on the Coquihalla and the news showed footage of cars on the shoulders all the way to the summit. We have chains for the truck but we'd rather not travel in snow.

The Fraser Valley is at once familiar and strange. I lived in this area as a child, on the other side of Sumas Mountain, and the flat vistas with mountains ringing the prairie strike a deep chord of memory. But the ridge of houses just east of Abbotsford is new; the subdivisions filling the fields where I remember cattle grazing make me realize how the heart balks at change in the recollections of childhood. Passing the Vedder River, I tell the children that this was where my horse was born, this was where I first came to look at him in a grassy field and my father knew it was impossible to do anything but buy him. They've seen pictures of that horse, a black Arabian gelding that I rode all through my teenage years and finally sold when I was a young woman wanting to travel.

At Chilliwack the word is that the Coquihalla is slushy and slow. We decide to take the Fraser Canyon Highway, intending to make Spences Bridge by nightfall. It's such a historic route, the Canyon, Yale with its old church and cairns telling of paddlewheelers and stagecoach lines. Edward Stout is buried here, his body scarred from an attack by Indians using arrows tipped with rattlesnake venom, north of Yale at Jackass Mountain. But that's not what killed him; he died of old age – ninety-nine years of it – after helping to discover Williams Creek and striking it rich in Barkerville. And at Spuzzum there's an old Indian cemetery on the delta, twenty skeletons buried in a sitting position around the remains of a fire.

All the tunnels and bars have their stories. Entering the darkness of the tunnels in late afternoon, we are cloaked with the memories of those who died in their making, names forgotten. We put on music to push back the gloomy twilight settling down on the highway – Nanci Griffith singing of the Great Divide and her delicate rendering of "Boots of Spanish Leather", Dylan himself accompanying her on harmonica. *There's nothing you can send me, my own true love. There's nothing I'm wishing to be owning. Just carry yourself back to me unspoiled, from across that lonesome ocean.* A train whistles somewhere nearby and we hear the sound of it passing in the dusk.

By five o'clock it is too dark to go on and an icy rain is falling so we decide to drive into Lytton to find a place to stay. A large house, sur-rounded by cottages, calls itself the Totem Motel and we are given one of the cottages for the night. It's a place out of time on its ridge above Fraser's river. The house is very old, surrounded by large trees, and our cottage has the smell of better days. Walking the dog, I pass more old houses and a firehall complete with antique fire engine parked to one side. Driving out later for a hamburger supper at the Jade Springs Restaurant, we pass the hospital and see patients sitting up in bed with meal trays across their laps and a nurse adjusting a lamp.

All through the night I am awakened by trains, this canyon a wide bowl of echoes, the sound of them haunting my dreams when I fall back to sleep.

THURSDAY, FEBRUARY 17

THIS IS A DAY for slow travel, stopping where we like to look at the country. It's bright and cold, yesterday's freezing rain leaving a glaze of black ice on the road to ensure the slow pace. We passed the sight of the Great Slide of August 13, 1905, when five natives, including Chief Lillooet, were buried alive as Arthur Seat Mountain slid down into the Thompson River, damming it for at least four hours. The impact as the slide hit the river caused a high wave that swept over the banks, drowning thirteen people. As we stopped to read the sign, I had the uncanny sense of knowing what it would say before I looked at it, and then realized I'd read of this before, in a pioneer memoir called *Widow Smith of Spences Bridge* that I'd recently finished.

It's the old Cariboo Wagon Road that winds down into Spences Bridge and we take it rather than staying on the Trans-Canada. The little town is quiet, children in school, a few businesses boarded up – for the winter or forever, we can't tell. The town is busy in the fall when fly-fishermen from all over congregate for the steelhead fishing. More than nineteen Indian villages were clustered in this area, the remains of dwellings hidden in sage, middens testifying to the historic significance of its fishery. Although I've never learned to fly-fish, the sight of the river rushing over gravel bars and the beauty of the Steelhead Inn, which I've read is one of the oldest continuously operating hotels in the province, are enough to determine me to learn.

Just north of Spences Bridge we stop to take a photograph of Great
Bluff. From the pull-out, squinting against the sun, I don't think it looks
much different than the famous photograph, taken in the 1860s, of a
covered wagon drawn by a mule-train passing through between the rock
bank on the west and the beak of rock on the river side of the road. In
the old photograph you can see the log sub-structure of the road and of
course today the road is wider, paved and flattened by millions of cars
over the years. But the hills beyond, fringed in places by pines and covered with bunchgrass, have the same timeless curve and below, the
Thompson moves towards its marriage with the Fraser, indifferent to the
centuries and traffic. We let the dog out for a pee and pick a few
branches of rabbit bush and sage to hang from the rearview mirror. The
smell fills the truck, reminding us all of summers past and camping trips
in this country. In my garden at home, in a dry corner, I have a couple
of these small grey plants, filched from a roadside, and even a tiny spec-
imen of the wild mock orange with its intense sweet blossoms. Before

The famous photograph of
Great Bluff, north of Spences
Bridge, circa *1865.*

we leave, the children count cars on a northbound train, waving to the engineer and having the thrill of hearing him sound his whistle in response. Beyond, we can see a tiny church huddled in the shadow of a talus slope, balanced in its angle of repose.

We've never driven off the main highway into Ashcroft so this time we do, through the dry hills to a lovely town on the banks of the river. We find a place to buy strong coffee, hot chocolate topped with whipped cream and cinnamon, and are told by the woman serving us not to miss the museum which she says is the best anywhere.

It is very good, in fact. Organized around the theme of old Ashcroft, it shows the visitor something of the pioneer past with displays of old farming equipment, beaded evening dresses for someone with an eighteen-inch waist, photographs of school groups and sports teams, evoking all the nostalgia typical of such displays. I would never have imagined that Ashcroft had been famous in its day for tomatoes and that Aylmer had a factory right here to process the ripe fruit. I think my favourite thing in the whole museum is the slide show picturing a whole selection of labels from canned tomatoes, some of them faintly familiar from my childhood. When we leave Ashcroft, I try to imagine where the tomato fields might have been among these pallid hills of sand and sagebrush, and why anyone would have let the rich soil necessary to the growing of tomatoes go back to sand, once established.

We had thought we might stay in Ashcroft, but cannot get the attention of the man sweeping the walkway along the second story of the only motel. So we drive on to Clinton, thinking there might be something there.

Clinton we know from driving north in summer; we've stopped here to buy pottery from a house on the side of the highway – three beautiful blue bowls, a pie-plate glazed in three colours, a casserole dish that cracked and broke the third time I used it. Clinton in summer is busy and friendly but as we drive into town, snow is falling fast and thick, and nothing is open but a small store where we stop to buy crusty rolls, ham, and orange juice, making a picnic in the truck as we drive south again in a blizzard.

Not wanting to drive forever, we find a room for the night in the cheapest motel in Cache Creek. It's hard to pry Brendan away from the television with TSN showing highlights of the winter Olympics but now that we have a place to stay, we want to go exploring along the Trans-Canada east to Kamloops. In particular we want to find Walhachin, which my parents have assured us we can drive to off this highway. A few miles east of Cache Creek we find a pull-off with a stop-of-interest sign telling of the ghosts of Walhachin.

The sign points southeast where nothing can be seen. Is this what my parents meant? I seem to remember them telling us about houses and so on but we can't see anything but hills, sagebrush, and the Thompson River. We keep going on the Trans-Canada east, thinking we remember a sign from years before, a simple road-sign pointing down a side road, saying Walhachin and maybe a distance: a few miles, no more. We drive as far as the provincial park at Juniper Beach and see nothing. Thinking that we can at least get some fishing in, we drive down to the park, deserted on this cold day in February. The campsites look lonely, the dog gets cactus barbs in her face and whimpers piteously as we take them out, there are a number of fish carcasses on the stones at the edge of the river, and a sign telling us that the river is closed to sport fishing at this time of year. There's a phone booth, though, and I call my parents in Victoria. My mother sounds stunned to hear my voice.

"I thought this was the week you were going away."

"I *am* away, Mum. I'm calling from Juniper Beach. We're trying to find Walhachin. You said it was on the west side of this park but we can't find anything. Is there something to see or just that sign on the highway?"

She tells me that there's a little village, you get there by taking the side road marked with a sign. Yes, she says, to the west of Juniper Beach. She says it twice, for emphasis.

"That settles it," says John. "Your mother always gets things wrong. We'll go east."

East we go and sure enough, a few miles down the highway there's a little marker saying simply Walhachin, 6 km. Right away, we know it's

'... The ground being opened for irrigation ditches, the horses leaning into their work ...' Walhachin, 1910.

something special. A trestle bridge, built in 1911, crosses the Thompson River by a huge plantation of ginseng and soon we're on the Anglesey Ranch Road. The Marquis of Anglesey, I remember, was one of the wealthy Englishmen that an entrepreneur had interested in the grand scheme of developing five thousand acres of arid land, planting fruit trees to be irrigated by an ambitious flume arrangement built in 1907 and coming thirty-two kilometers from Deadman River. A certain type of aristocratic settler was encouraged, those who would appreciate the merits of polo and who would understand the necessity of dressing formally for dinner. Balls would take place at the posh Walhachin Hotel and I've seen a photograph of it, a gracious building with a man lounging on a lush lawn, a small dog at his side, and two women demure in long dresses. I've also seen a photograph of the ground being opened for irrigation ditches, the horses leaning into their work and thick dust rising from their feet, and another of vast plowed fields, seeded with something, and a final photograph of a man in a suit holding up a huge clump of potatoes. In *Widow Smith of Spences Bridge*, I remember Mrs. Smith commenting on the lovely crops of apples that the settlers were harvesting at Walhachin and how sad it was to see the trees wither and die after the men failed to come home from World War I. I've read that the flume was destroyed in a storm and also that it had been poorly constructed to begin with, of green lumber, the upper-class farmers of Walhachin unaccustomed to seeking or taking advice on anything.

This is all in my mind as we drive up onto the bench of land above the Thompson River and see what's left of that romantic community. There are several of the original houses, one of riverstone, one or two of weathered wood. We drive to one end of the site and back, seeing road-signs indicating *Sunnymeade Square, Magner Street, Wilkinson Street, Thompson Crescent*. These suggest gracious avenues that might once have existed but no longer do. Mostly present-day Walhachin consists of some mobile homes, a good deal of rubble, a pretty post-office with a sign in its plant-filled window saying CLOSED and a Union Jack fluttering above. But the air is so dry and clear that I feel a stirring of understanding: the *why* of this place, this sky, this long grassy benchland. One old house is in the throes of renovation, new french doors opening onto a view of the river. A few lilacs flourish in the front yard and there are stakes for something else, delphiniums maybe, come June. I wonder where the water comes from now. On our way out to the highway I can see some weathered remains of the flume riding the side of the hill.

One guidebook that we have tells of hoodoos up the Deadman River road so we turn there and find ourselves heading north into a narrow canyon lined with ranches crouched low under cottonwoods, and horse dung in frequent piles along the road. The river has obviously rerouted itself more then a few times; we see signs of the banks having caved in and high dry beds which might once have held water. I know from Mark Hume's book, *The Run of the River*, that this is the spawning creek of the Thompson River steelhead and the run is in danger from these ranches and the means they use to irrigate their land. Somehow I can't imagine those big fish in this dark chasm, pushing their way up the tea-coloured water, under the brooding hoodoos that are so hidden in the late afternoon light we're not sure we see them. Coming back to the highway, we stop for a small tribe of horses, taking their time, sniffing the wind before heading up a trail towards the derelict flume.

Tonight we eat in the dining room of the Travelodge in Cache Creek. Immaculate linen, tomato juice in little glasses, improbable bouquets of flowers that turn out to be silk, and food that might have come from a menu unchanged for twenty years – grilled cheese on white bread, garnished with a pickle, lamb chops with frozen diced vegetables and a packet of Kraft mint jelly, a salmon steak served with an aging wedge of lemon. We walk back in hail to our motel where I fall asleep to the plummy accent of *Rumpole of the Bailey* on the TV.

Friday, February 18

WE CAN'T WAIT to leave when we all wake before seven. All last night the big rigs rushed down the highway nearby, bent on Vancouver before first light. One child walks the dog down behind the 24-hour grocery where there are at least a few tufts of grass for her to pee on, and the rest of us pack up quickly. We drive back to Ashcroft where a convenience store is open and I buy some pastries to supplement our granola bars and fruit, as well as a couple of huge cups of coffee to pour into the thermos. Ashcroft is still lovely in the early light and a few gaffers are talking of cattle by the coffee machine. We could be a hundred miles from Cache Creek instead of ten or so.

We decide to take the Highland Valley Road over to Logan Lake and then follow the old road running adjacent to Guichon Creek all the way down to Merritt. The Highland Valley Road rises high above Ashcroft and winds through glorious country. The views are spectacular, snowy hills and wide-open grassland all the way to the Coast Range. I've never seen such devastation done to a landscape as that by the copper mine we pass towards Logan Lake, an entire mountain taken apart and sludge pools all around, the same colour as the verdigris on my copper coffee pot at home. A few enormous earth movers sit on the hill.

We stop in Logan Lake to give the dog a break. In front of the recreation centre there's one of the huge earth movers, with a proud sign announcing that it has been donated by the copper mine to the people of Logan Lake. Oh boy, I thought, what a gift. *Ah, but I just thought you might be wanting something fine, made of silver or of golden.* A piece of mining equipment, anchored to the parking lot, capable of moving mountains in its day.

We reach Merritt early and buy picnic food at the Overwaitea to take out to Monck Park on Nicola Lake. By now the sun is warm and we want to be outside. The sign at the Monck Park turn-off says the park is closed for the season but we drive on anyway, hoping that the gates are open. And they are. We hike up on the hill where we hike in summer, the air pungent with pine resin and the grey herbs. We can see Quilchena across the lake and the hills above where we drive in summer to watch sunsets, sitting among blue flax and brown-eyed Susans. This is what we came for, I think to myself, and then say it out loud. Everyone agrees.

We eat down by the lake, sunflower seed rolls, cheese, meat, fruit, pistachios, and cookies, and finish the last of the coffee from Ashcroft. It's hot, though we know the weather can change as suddenly as the wide sky, and I'm not surprised to see that my children are playing on clumps of ice washed up on the shore. Then they take turns rolling into the kikuli pits while John and I lie under sheltering pines and read the newspaper. *The same thing I would want today, I would want again tomorrow.*

On the drive out, we see an osprey sitting in a tree by the lake, a western meadowlark, and then suddenly we're in the middle of a huddle of cows, some with new calves, precarious on stilty legs. This is what we miss in the summers because the cattle are all up on their summer range, but right now they are down here calving. It is so lovely, all the new mothers contentedly standing in warm grass with their young nuzzling their milk bags or else bawling. Some cows stand off alone, looking preoccupied, and I tell the children that I think these ones are about to calve because I remember this behaviour from my earlier years on a dairy farm. We drive slowly, windows open, calling *Well done!* and *Congratulations!* to the nearest mothers.

Back at Merritt we find a motel with a kitchenette and two bedrooms, bring in our gear, and then head downtown to poke in shops. In the bookstore there are always unexpected surprises – this time, a book about King Arthur, a history of BC in archival photographs, a journal of a writer's year in a small Wiltshire village, and a wonderful collection of Donald Hall's essays about country living. Brendan buys a basketball and wants to get back to the motel to shoot baskets in a hoop he saw in the parking lot.

Tonight we'll eat spaghetti with garlic bread, and ice cream for dessert. Each of us will have a bed and we will be in Merritt, which we love.

SATURDAY, FEBRUARY 19

OUR MISTAKE IN CHOOSING this motel is evident at 1 a.m. when the clientele of the Valnicola Pub across the road spill out onto the street for a fight. I keep thinking they'll discover the open window of the room where John and I are lying awake and ... do what? Punch us? But we don't close the window because it is too stuffy without fresh air. Soon we hear the sirens of police cars streaming down from the detachment up on the ridge and eventually, after many shouts and threats, it is quiet enough to fall back to sleep.

Today is fine and warm so we head back out to the park for another hike, coming back to Merritt in time for the public skate at the arena just across the way. We've brought skates because I had the foolish idea that we'd just find frozen lakes strung out along this trip like jewels. Instead, we go to the Merritt Arena which is so much like the places I spent hours in as a girl watching my brothers play hockey. We love it, though, because there are hardly any people, the music is country and western, Rosanne Cash and Vince Gill singing "We don't need those memories hanging 'round," and our children, new to skating this winter, are clearly in heaven as they race around the ice. I go back to the motel early to make soup and sandwiches for their return.

We drive out to Quilchena in the late afternoon. Nanci Griffith still sings, though the kids ask for something else. But this song suits me fine – *Oh, I might be gone a long old time, and it's only that I'm asking. Is there something I can send you to remember me by, to make your time more easy passing?* By now a cold wind is blowing up off the lake but the kids still want ice cream in the general store. And I want something, too, though I don't know what it is. I buy an enamelled blue coffeepot because the copper one at home has lost its handle – and I lose my heart to boots. These are no ordinary boots but red Laredo boots, sitting on the shelf with the purple ones, the green ones, the regular browns and blacks. If they weren't $175 I'd try them on in a minute, but as it is they are just a fancy. Oh I could do things in these boots, do anything, climb, dance, walk for miles. The lady who works in the store asks us where we've come from and seems surprised that we are so familiar with the area. We tell her we come every summer and we just wanted to see the country in winter. We talk about the changes over the years and then she asks me if I like Ian Tyson. Out of the blue.

"He comes to Douglas Lake every summer, you know."

I assure her that I love Ian Tyson, particularly "And Stood There Amazed."

"Then I'll give you the Douglas Lake number and you should phone early for tickets. The barn only holds eight hundred and the tickets go fast."

I thank her and we drive back to Merritt, two children asleep in the back and the other quiet. I am thinking of the boots. I could wear them to the Ian Tyson dance and maybe waltz in the arms of a cowboy. At the motel, we eat hamburgers and salad and go to bed early, our sleep broken this night by a group of men in the next room who sound like they're bouncing basketballs off the walls until the small hours.

WE WAKE TO SNOW and John swears strongly, thinking of our trip home over the Coquihalla, the chains unopened in the back. We try to get road conditions on the weather channel but can find nothing for this area. We pack up and eat breakfast at the ABC, large plates of bacon and eggs, hashbrowns and toast, telling the children this might have to do for hours so eat everything.

The snow has stopped by the time we finish breakfast and we head up the Coquihalla, which is sanded and mostly bare, but the drifts of snow on the sides of the road are higher than our truck. On some banks we can see the prints of animals, elk maybe, and certainly rabbits with the telltale drag of the leg. It is gloriously sunny and the ride through the pass is wonderful, the mountains rising around us and the glaciers brilliant in sunlight.

We stop at Fort Langley because Brendan has been studying the fur trade at school. I haven't been here in years and look forward to showing my children the cooperage, the factor's house, the press that made compact bundles of the furs. Unfortunately a Cub and Brownie jamboree is just setting up on the grounds and the man making barrels tells us that over a thousand participants are expected. The chance for the past to shimmer in the air like a curtain for us to pass through is lost as hordes of excited kids in familiar camp hats rush from building to building on their quest for badges, then hot dogs. We eat our lunch outside the fort, setting our food on the tailgate of our truck, and then begin the drive into Vancouver and over the Lions Gate Bridge to the ferry.

ON THE FERRY FROM HORSESHOE BAY
TO LANGDALE, THAT SAME DAY

WHILE THE CHILDREN WALK the decks to stretch their legs after a long day's drive, I am sitting with this notebook to make sure I haven't forgotten anything. Of course I have because I see I haven't mentioned trying on a Lee jean jacket in the Fields store in Merritt or looking at the photograph in the Ashcroft Museum of the couple from the Upper Hat Creek Valley, he holding a cigarette and she, a cat in her arms. Who were they and where did they end up? Behind them you can see the evidence of hayfields and tall cottonwoods to picnic under when the work is finished. They look so young and proud in the air of 1913, before the War, before the fire that burned down most of Ashcroft, before the young men left nearby Walhachin for battles they'd never return from. We've taken lots of photographs, of course, and will put them in our album to tell something of this ramble. The truck still smells of sage, though the sprig hanging from the mirror is withered and dry. And every time I hear Nanci Griffith sing, I'll regret that I didn't at least try on the red Laredo boots:

Minta and Walter Pocock,
Upper Hat Creek Valley.

> *Take heed, take heed of the western wind.*
> *Take heed of stormy weather.*
> *And yes, there is something you can send back to*
>   *me.*
> *Send me boots of Spanish leather.*

The Road
to Bella Coola

How shall the heart be reconciled to its feast of losses?
                                          – Stanley Kunitz, "The Layers"

FOUR DAYS BEFORE we left for our summer camping trip, I went to your memorial service. I took Forrest and Angelica; Forrest was already out of school for the summer and we picked up Angelica at lunch hour. It was also the afternoon of Brendan's class party so I didn't even give him a choice. It seemed wrong for him to miss the hamburgers and ice cream sundaes, the chance to practise the jive and another dance his teacher had spent some time teaching them for this end-of-the-year Fifties party. You'd said to bring the children if I thought it wouldn't trouble them too much. And Brendan would have come if there had been a choice because he loved you in a deep, wordless way. Talking of you, his eyes would fill up with tears and he'd look away. He wanted to know what would happen to your body and I told him how you'd chosen what you'd wear for your cremation – a white cotton nightie and slippers your kids had given you for Christmas, and in your ears, golden hoops from your sister.

At your service, people gathered on the lawn among your trees and flowers. Your gentle labrador looked lost, wandering around the fringes, watching for you. Your sister asked us to follow the family up the Rock, the place where you loved to sit, a high sudden knoll, with a hard way up, and an easier way. We all followed by the easier route, past the pale yellow ribbons tied to broom and ocean spray. Your chair was up there, with Ray's, and on the seat of yours was the blue jug with white polka dots that had been your grandmother's, filled with flowers. People spoke of you, your sister, your nephews, your brother-in-law, your daughter, your friend Joanne, and I did too. My children cried as I read the little eulogy I'd prepared, and when I sat down we shared my kleenex. All of us left the Rock and your family stayed for awhile, to release you or say a private final goodbye. There was keening and the sound of a drum. My daughter asked what the yellow ribbons were for and I told her that yellow meant remembrance and I sang her a little of the song about yellow ribbons on oak trees, standing for loyalty and faithfulness.

The next few days were so busy, John and I getting all our camping gear out and packing boxes, the tent-trailer, and the back of the truck, and attending the ceremonies marking the end of the school year. People came for meals in the midst of it all and there was the garden to water, potted plants to put in big tubs so that they wouldn't dry out while we were away. At night I was so tired I fell into heavy sleep, never dreaming. It wasn't until we were on the road, driving up towards Ashcroft and Spences Bridge, that I began to grieve for you more deeply than I thought I could bear. I hadn't thought it would be like that. I thought I'd hurt once, badly, and then it would diminish, a little each day. Then I remembered the words of Claudius, in Hamlet, talking to his wife of the death of Ophelia's father and the daughter's subsequent madness: *O Gertrude, Gertrude, / When sorrows come, they come not single spies / But in battalions.* And later, telling Laertes of Ophelia's death, Gertrude laments, *One woe doth tread upon another's heel, / So fast they follow.* For me, there was just one death, yours, and the fact of it sinking into my heart again and again.

At Skihist that first night, I dreamed of you. There were things I wanted to tell you and I knew I never could; things I wanted to ask you, like the name of the pale lilac flower on the old wagon road leading south from the campsite towards Lytton, or what animal's scat it was we'd found, flecked with rose hips. In the dream you were coming on the trip with us yet you carried no luggage, took up no room at all.

By noon the next day it was raining. It rained the whole time we stayed with my brother and his family in the Nazko Valley, west of Quesnel, and the whole time at Barkerville after that. I remembered you telling me that you'd sent to Barkerville for English willow plates from the Mason and Daly store to cheer you up one blue winter. So much there reminded me of you – the table linens edged with Cluny lace, wreathes of twisted dried willow. I almost bought a postcard to send to you – Barkerville with an ominous sky overhead. I even had a clever thing to say on it. Then I was pierced with such remorse for forgetting you'd died.

On the way out from Barkerville, we stopped at Cottonwood House. It was not yet ten o'clock and a woman was just opening up for the day. A hutch of bunnies sheltered in the lee of a tool shed, ducks stood around as though thinking about something important, and two lambs followed our movements up and down the length of their fence. The woman told us they were not long for the world and would soon be bound for the freezer of a man who cared for the stock. The fields surrounding the farm were ripe with tall grasses, barn swallows dipped and called, entering their nests on high beams of the breezeway between the barns where their young waited with open beaks. The woman took us through the house and every room gave me pleasure – the bedrooms with their quilts (faded Dresden plates for the family and bright serviceable patchworks of plaid flannel and red homespun for the drovers and miners who would stop for the night) and the kitchen with its enamel sinks and wonderful stove, gleaming copper and big yellowware bowls for bread or puddings. So much of what I saw was filtered through the sense I had that you would have loved it, you would have wanted a kitchen just like it. The lambs by the back door bleated so insistently that we went into their paddock to rub their heads to console them.

We'd never driven Highway 20 before and it was one focus for this trip, if the weather was suitable and our tempers survived the first week of camping. At Williams Lake we checked the tires, the oil, filled our jugs with water, and headed west, up the long rise into the Chilcotin. I hadn't expected such vistas – the Fraser, the wide grasslands, ridges of pines and trembling aspen. We camped the first night on the edge of the Chilcotin River, behind a split-rail fence. Not since northern Utah had I seen a river that colour, milky green, like celadon. A little way from our campsite I found bear scat among the fleabane and southernwood, and further on, a simple trail down the bank to the river, littered with deer droppings. John and Forrest cast the requisite barbless hooks into the river to try to land us supper, but lost a rainbow as it broke the surface of the water on its way in. All around us wildflowers nodded and tossed in the warm wind – wild roses, yarrow, arnica, and pale yellow salsify. And low junipers, studded with berries that smelled of gin when pinched. We'd have talked about this, I know; I'd have wanted to get the softness of this landscape just right for you, the way the dust settled on the fine hairs of our arms as we walked back from the pump with jugs of cold water, the smell of the air, the haze of stars, and the tired log cabins collapsing back into grass.

We drove all the way to Bella Coola the next day, stopping just west of Anahim Lake for a picnic by a sluggish creek. Too late – we already had the food out, the dog was down in the creek – we discovered it to be a major breeding centre for mosquitoes that stung us everywhere, right through our clothing. You'd have laughed as I described our dance, sandwiches in one hand, apples in the other, trying to keep the mosquitoes at bay. A truck paused, thinking us in trouble, then sped up quickly without a backward glance. We kept expecting to see bears but didn't, not even in Tweedsmuir Park, where the signs all warned sternly of their presence, grizzlies and blacks. A few deer, a muskrat swimming across a slough, leaving a wedge of ripples behind it, a small grey animal we couldn't identify, and lots of ducks. There was nowhere to camp in Tweedsmuir. Every site was full of tents, with fishing poles leaning against them, or else campers and motorhomes caked with the mud of the road. We began our descent to the Bella Coola Valley, down a switchback road called the Hill, more like a goat track, following an eighteen percent grade down the mountainside. There were no guardrails or abutments to prevent us from tumbling off the side of the mountain and into the waters of the Bella Coola River which we could see far below. We stopped to let the brakes cool and Brendan tossed a rock over the edge; we heard it splash as it entered the river. A brochure we'd picked up somewhere stressed that there had been no fatal accidents on the Hill, although I remember reading about a man who'd gone over and had got hung up in a tree some distance below. I couldn't stop myself from looking down, although I felt dizzy and held on tight to the arm rest of the truck. Someone had told us that camping in the valley was no problem, you just pulled off the road wherever you wanted. So once we'd reached the foot of the Hill, we began to think about a place to stop for the night.

We drove through Firvale and Hagensborg, admiring the tidy farms in the shadow of mountains. We found just one campsite, which was full, and we couldn't imagine stopping on the side of the road which was busier than we'd thought it would be. We decided to splurge on a motel for the night. There were two in Bella Coola proper. One was small with rooms directly over the pub. John and I looked at each other and tried to find the second one, advertised on a billboard coming into the town as having kitchen units. We had pork chops in the cooler that needed to be cooked. But that one was full. We went back onto the main road to find a place to pull over, maybe a clearing or an abandoned farm. We ended up on a road leading to a Forestry Recreation Area up the Nusatsum River; the road was tarry with fresh bear dung and when we stopped to let the dog stretch her legs, she began to whimper and moan. A family in a camper truck going in the opposite direction stopped to tell us that the campsite was three picnic tables under some trees in a bug-infested marsh. The woman rolled her eyes and looked as though she'd been crying.

"How far?" we asked, feeling as though we had no choice.

"Just past the twenty-five-kilometre post," the man said, rolling up his window against mosquitoes.

We were at the nine-kilometre post and the road was really climbing, parts of it washed away. So we headed back to Hagensborg where we'd seen another motel, pub adjacent this time, and checked in, buying ice at the store across the road to chill our pork chops for one more night. We ate in Bella Coola and I kept thinking that this would make a good story for you – the restaurant with stained seats that served a fabulous seafood Newburg in a haze of cigarette smoke under a stained glass head of Tutankhamen; the Greenpeace boat coming in at the government wharf and a contingent of Nuxalk natives greeting it in their button blankets and ceremonial headdresses; those mountains everywhere, and the sound of water.

If geography is one way we have of locating ourselves in the land, then I was lost on the road to Bella Coola. When my son threw his stone down off the mountain into the green river below, I felt my heart sink too. I was farther and farther away from you, the glaciers cold and aloof in their high distance. At Skihist, I could dream you into our camp, your presence at home in the tawny grass. Once, you and Ray drove all the way to Spences Bridge to look at some logs you thought you might use for the house you were renovating. You loved the sage, the dry air, the long road home through the Canyon.

Driving back on Highway 20, I kept noticing the graveyards – in Redstone, Tatla Lake, Alexis Creek. In one, on a reserve, there were weathered crosses and one painted bright purple and then, strangely out of place, a spirit house. I didn't think the Chilcotin Indians built spirit houses for their dead. But when we were visiting my brother in Nazko, there was a funeral for one of the elders of the Nazko band, and a whole bus load of mourners came from Anahim Lake for the ceremony. It turned out the woman who died had been born in the Chilcotin and had married a Carrier man, so it's likely there had been other marriages between the two tribes, other deaths. My brother's wife said that meat was burned each Friday in the graveyards for the ancestors' nourishment. I found the sight of the spirit house comforting. It gave a form for one's grief, a place to focus one's sorrow. I thought of the pain your family must be feeling, each day, in your house, surrounded by your pictures and crockery, the loveliness of your spirit all around them to remind them of what they'd known and lost.

Except I don't think that your spirit is lost to us, exactly. That's what makes your death so painful. Enough of you is here, and tangible, your ideas, what you did and meant, so that we feel the absence of you even more acutely. Five days before you died, I visited you for the last time. You were entirely confined to your bed and thin, so thin that I wanted to cry. We'd always joked about our weight and I said to you, What a way to get skinny! You smiled, your smile still intact although your face was fading away, almost transparent. You said you were afraid but ready. I went out to your garden and cut you some moss roses from the bush I'd rooted for you from mine. Then we cleaned out your purse, so your husband wouldn't have to do it, and you sent it home with me because I'd always liked it. I meant to carry it on this trip, not knowing you'd be dead by the time we left, dead and ashes with farewells said sadly on the Rock. Somehow I couldn't, it still smelled of you, and I just wanted to put your dying into a different context before I used it. Empty purse, body emptied of spirit, house without you in it. Coming down off the Chilcotin Plateau, we played the Bruce Cockburn tape with the song that I think of as your elegy: *Death's no stranger, stranger than the life I've seen … Gone from mystery into mystery, gone from daylight into night, another step deeper into darkness, closer to the light.*

We went on to the Cariboo after the Chilcotin, then to the Nicola Valley where you had once lived. In the past, you and I had compared notes about what we liked best in the area. For me, it was standing up on the volcanic slope on the west side of Nicola Lake, looking over at Quilchena, the hills shadowed by clouds and the dust of a truck coming fast down the Pennask Lake Road. You liked driving north on 5A towards Kamloops, in the days when you and Ray were courting, with the windows open and the smell of sage coming in. I did both things this time, stood looking to Quilchena and drove north on 5A. I sat at the picnic table after the children had run down to the lake for a swim and watched a nuthatch winding down the trunk of a pine, utterly unafraid of me, and I listened carefully to the querulous crows at dawn, thinking it might be a code. The morning after you died, I woke before sunrise to hear voices, throaty and rough, and instead of being afraid, I went outside to see who it was. Two huge ravens were sitting on the peak of the roof, talking to another sitting a few yards away in a big cedar. I leaned on the deck rail and listened, hoping to hear something of you. In the old stories, Raven stole light, foretold the weather, the arrival of visitors, and imminent death. I think they might still be messengers because these ones inclined their heads towards me, to make sure I was listening. I only wish I could have understood.

In the past, I'd always come to you soon after a ramble, wanting to tell you things I'd seen and done because, in telling you, I found ways to see the best of my life. You'd tell me how lovely it all sounded, how lucky I was, and I'd forget the nights of lying awake in a tent, holding a child with an earache, miles from a doctor, or cooking the umpteenth meal on the Coleman stove in rain, the long drives over bumpy roads to find whatever it was we sought. I'd try for the clearest way to say what it was I found in the hills above Nicola Lake, at Walhachin, on the streets of Barkerville at dusk with a trailing note of dulcimer still hanging in the air, fragile as gossamer. You were like a nourishment, rich and necessary. I feel desolate to think we'll not talk again.

On the road to Bella Coola, I saw everything twice, once for myself and once for you. The purple vetch, hawkweed, smell of sunlight on river rock, pine sap, and the unbearable sweetness of wild roses crowding the path to the water pump, all garlanded by golden asters, shining arnica, salsify the colour of your ribbons. Sorrow is a keen companion, hunting the roadsides and skies for images to hold the memory of a beloved spirit, light as pollen in warm wind off the river.

Sunlight
on Canvas

WE CAMPED FOR TWO WEEKS, roaming the province in search of good weather. When we found it at Lac La Hache after a week of two nights here, one night there, we decided we'd stay a couple of nights to dry out our stuff and wash some clothes at the laundromat listed on the park information sign as being right across the road on the way to the public beach. We'd stayed in this campsite once before, en route to Barkerville, and it wasn't exactly prized in our memories. At night we'd hear the logging trucks heading south at an astonishing speed, the lake had swimmer's itch, and it was neither here nor there as far as location was concerned. But this time I welcomed the chance to relax with a book while the kids explored, and to sleep in past seven in the morning, nudging John out the door to make coffee, which he brought to me in bed. I drank it while listening to loons on the lake.

Since our children were small, my husband and I have taken them camping each summer, sometimes far afield, sometimes just across Jervis Inlet from our home on the north end of the Sechelt Peninsula. In some ways, this is probably an attempt to recover our own childhood summers. John's family would head for the Rockies from wherever they were living – Winnipeg, Calgary, Coquitlam. My family would strike out for lakes where my father could fish or else we'd pile into the station wagon to find places my father had read about that winter: sites of the Riel Rebellion; rivers visionary priests drifted down to educate the Indians; the Plains of Abraham. Once, we drove clear across Canada to Halifax so that my father could take up a new posting in his naval career, and two years later we drove back to Vancouver Island. We camped on those two journeys, stopping once or twice to stay with friends or relations so that my mother could do laundry.

My family had a blue tent, peaked, with an extension out behind it. We all slept in it, my brothers and me in our identical sleeping bags, nylon with blue plaid flannel linings, and our parents in two bags, zipped together. The dog slept inside, too, near the door. There was also a pink plastic chamber pot which we'd pee in if we woke in the night, needing to. More than once it was knocked over by the dog or by one of us. Our air mattresses never stayed comfortable. No matter what, no matter that my father carefully identified where the leak was, and fixed it, no matter that he carved new toggles to fit snugly into the leaking valves, no more than one or two of the air mattresses remained inflated for a whole night. My mother cooked meals in an old black skillet and a dented aluminum saucepan. We ate fish as often as my father could catch it, fried crisply in a cornmeal coating, and mounds of instant mashed potatoes with a lump of butter melting in the centre.

Our camping equipment is rather more complicated. We have a tent-trailer which my parents spotted in a lot in Colwood, near Victoria. We'd mentioned to them that we thought we might like a tent-trailer, and then decided against buying one because we couldn't afford to spend any more money than we had already spent on camping paraphernalia. They phoned us to tell us they'd found the ideal rig for us and we demurred, saying we'd changed our minds about buying one. There was silence on their end of the phone line and then my father confessed that they'd been so sure we'd love this tent-trailer that they put a down payment on it in our name, offering exactly what the dealer was asking;

we could pay them back at our leisure. So what could we do but take the ferry to Victoria to pick it up? The dealer turned out to be shady, having set up on part of a service-station lot with a few trailers and a hand-lettered sign. He was missing a number of fingers on both hands and couldn't be located later when we discovered a few problems with the tent-trailer, not the least of which was the fact that it shared its serial number and registration papers with three others trailers; this last was told to us sternly by someone from ICBC. So this is what we camp in. It sleeps three of us, having a double bed and a single, and the remaining two sleep in a small tent when it's fine and in the back of the truck when it's raining. The configurations vary. My husband and I speak of ourselves "sleeping in the tent" when we want privacy a few days into the camping trip. Whichever kids are currently getting along are the two that sleep in the same area with the odd man out in the tent-trailer's single bed. We use a Coleman stove to cook on and a cooler with blocks of ice for our food, the tent-trailer not being the sort with propane or a sink or anything fancy.

It occurred to me at Lac La Hache that almost nobody camps in tents anymore, at least not in the sort of provincial park that I think of as a stopover rather than a destination. We arrived mid-afternoon and the campsite was more than half empty. We set up our tent and tent-trailer, went for a swim, towelled off vigourously to prevent swimmer's itch (as recommended on the big sign by the beach), and returned to make dinner. By eight, as the kids roasted marshmallows over a good fire, people were starting to appear off the highway. Big motorhomes, trucks with campers, and trucks pulling fifth wheels and trailers. They'd cruise up and down the little roads, backing into sites with a fair amount of effort – we'd hear men yelling from the driver's seat at their wives, who'd be standing in the middle of the pull-in making uncertain hand-signals in the falling light. Then we'd hear the buzz of pumps and generators, and the sound of radios, and I'd see the glow of televisions as I took the dog for her evening constitutional. There were exceptions, of course. A family from California across from us, for instance. They had a tent, a big one. We saw the two daughters walking to the washroom at bedtime, one in a pink nightdress, one in white. Their mother stood in a pastel dressing gown, prodding the fire. It was a bit like a sleep-over. We noticed that people would stare into our campsite as they passed, right into the tent, in fact, where I'd be stretched out with a book. Some would nod encouragingly, as if to say, "We're all in this together." Most just stared, taking in the worn canvas on the tent-trailer, the battered Coleman, fishing gear out to be sorted or repaired, the dog tied to a convenient tree. At meal times, they'd slow down and try to figure out what we were eating. In the washrooms, I'd see women setting and styling their hair, letting a facial mask harden on their skin, doing their nails and letting them dry under a blast of air from the hand drier. I was particularly interested in the German tourists because their toilet routines were amazing. They'd walk briskly to the washrooms in smart outfits, sweaters artfully draped over the shoulders, carrying hairdriers and Water-Piks complete with voltage adapters. They'd perform elaborate ablutions, all smiles, with one or two well-practised conversational openers, usually involving bears. They were always so clean, with gleaming teeth and tanned burnished skin. I felt like the lesser sister, troll of the woods, in my soiled t-shirt, mosquito bites all over my arms, and my hair untidily braided. I kept spraying tea-rose cologne down my shirt so at least I wouldn't smell.

In Tweedsmuir Park there were lots of tents, so many tents that we couldn't find a place for our own and had to go elsewhere. This was a place people hiked from, some of them following Mackenzie's route to the Pacific, exploring glaciers, and photographing mountain wall-flowers and moss campion in the high alpine meadows. Tweedsmuir reminded me a little of Glacier National Park, where we stayed a few years ago on our way to the badlands. People ranged out into the wilderness all around, hiking, climbing, fishing. They'd cache their food in the trees, sit around the fire at night with the mountains in their eyes; in their packs, worn annotated guides to wildflowers and birds.

At Lac La Hache, the laundromat turned out to be part of a phony operation with a campsite of its own, billed as "historical" for some reason beyond my grasp. When asked about laundry, the fat woman in a wheelchair behind the counter of the store looked irritated and said, when I told her I'd come from the provincial site, "Well, that's the problem. *Our* campers have to have access to the washing machine before anyone else." Never mind that campers from the provincial site passed the tawdry store each time they went to the public beach, stopping in for ice cream, pop, overpriced groceries, and secondhand books marked as new. I washed out t-shirts and underpants by hand in the salad bowl, hanging them on rope strung from tree to tree.

When we were camped at Bull Canyon, earlier in the same trip, we'd hung our sleeping bags, heavy sweaters, and damp jeans across a split-rail fence separating our campsite from the milky green Chilcotin River. In that provincial park, everyone – and there were only three other groups – kept to themselves, wanting the pleasure of the warm air, the wildflowers, and the singular rush of the river, not the chatter of strangers. I sat on a fence rail, watching my husband and son fish. I wanted to see deer come down off the hill on the other side of the river to drink, wanted to see a hawk return to the nest I thought I could detect in the pines, a mouse or snake clutched in its beak for the hungry nestlings. I felt as though I was somewhere, a place where Nature continued in its cadence, oblivious to my presence.

Lac La Hache boasted the Wagon Road Interpretive Trail, a two-kilometre walk with signposts telling something of the stories and ecology of the park. I usually like these trails, having walked the Last Mile to Richfield, learning a little about geology and placer mining, and having a sense of what it must have looked like with the early claims, the schoolhouse, the sad path leading to the Chinese cemetery. At Pacific Rim National Park, I liked the Rainforest Trail and the Shorepine Bog Trail, both with their useful booklets containing specific and accurate information about plants and ecosystems. The Wagon Road Trail was a disappointment. The most interesting thing, large numbers of Columbia lilies (a plant I knew was an important food source for the Indians), went unnoted. Signpost 3 told of the Blue Tent Ranch, a roadhouse flourishing during the 1860s, but there was nothing of it remaining, apart from a few stumps. Another signpost called itself Windy Crossing and said that the stand of trees around it, mostly Douglas firs, were well adapted to wind. The most startling of all was a signpost with the accompanying note: *Frozen Flying Fish? Don't be too surprised if you find a fish on the forest floor! The Lac La Hache area is home to many predator birds, such as the bald eagle, osprey and red-tailed hawk.* "That's really pushing it," said John, laughing. "I guess they couldn't find anything else to say." Clouds of mosquitoes followed us the entire walk.

When I was a child, my family sometimes camped at Englishman River. To get to that park, you turned off the main highway from Parksville to Port Alberni and drove through farmland in the shadow of Mount Arrowsmith. The campsite was always cool, sheltered by huge trees, with the river running through it, deep green pools and white falls singing you to sleep each night, familiar as a lullaby. It seems to me now that everyone had tents then, and the woods were lovely at dusk, the peaked canvas roofs gilded by the last light. You could smell cooking in those days; pork and beans, Kraft dinner, the occasional savoury stew. Sometimes a sleek Airstream trailer pulled by a big car with California plates would cruise the park and my mother would sigh as she washed the melmac dishes in an old plastic pan. My father would be off in search of the ideal fishing hole and my brothers and I would have teamed up with other kids in the campsite to play a game of tracking. This was glorified hide-and-seek. You divide into two teams, one remaining in a designated spot while the other team proceeds to hide, leaving an elaborate system of tracks behind: arrows fashioned from sticks; outlined footprints in the gravel, articulated with pebbles; bits of witches' hair threaded on the ends of branches. It seemed a universal code that we all knew, perhaps from Boy Scouts and Girl Guides, which everyone belonged to in those days. It was thrilling to crouch behind a huge cedar log that smelled of fungus and rotting bark, waiting for the other team to read the signs and discover you. We played this game until it was too dark to see the tracks, walking back over the suspension bridge to our campsite, hoping that this would go on and on. If my children meet other kids in campsites, it always seems to be to ride bikes up and down the roads. When I suggest that they play tracking, they look at me as though I'm speaking another language, which I suppose I am.

On this trip, we spent a night at Skihist, another provincial park I remember from childhood. We stayed there en route to Alberta in the days before the Coquihalla when you either drove north to Cache Creek and then east on the Trans-Canada or else you took the Crows-nest route over the Hope-Princeton. Skihist hasn't changed much, apart from flush toilets and taps for water. We set up our tent and tent-trailer for the good view west to Stein Mountain and slept with the sound of trains passing all night along the Thompson River. Although it's a stopover site, not unlike Lac La Hache, Skihist has the aura of a place that has known significant history. The Cariboo Wagon Road passed through here, men on foot leading mules laden with equipment, bull-slingers driving their oxen teams pulling freight wagons north to the gold fields. And on the benches above the river, Indians picking balsam root and native tobacco. The air was pungent with pine, southernwood, wild mock orange in season, and the light had an unearthly clarity. I can't remember if I walked the remnants of the Wagon Road when I was a child but we walked it this time, our shadows passing down the long slope of bunchgrass into memory.

I wonder what it is that keeps us on the road, summer after summer, drifting through the province, because in retrospect the mundane far exceeds perfection. Campfires, maybe, with all their forms and pur-poses. A campfire coaxed to burn in rain, intended to keep bugs away, is completely different from a campfire using dry pine needles as tinder, in say the Nicola Valley, intended for marshmallows and a sundowner of whiskey as you look east to the high grazing country beyond Quilchena. When I pack the boxes for camping, my children shriek, "Oh boy, marshmallows," and I know they're anticipating the fire, the peeled sticks, and gusts of smoke as the wind changes. I've loved going to bed in the tent with the last smoke penetrating the walls, and waking in the morning to the smell of a new fire, kindled against the chill of the air.

Sunlight on canvas, pine smoke – what do the people in the huge motorhomes smell at bedtime, and waking? When they're watching the late news on television, the doormat of astroturf becoming damp with dew, we're trying to figure out compass points by the position of the stars or listening to the nighthawks whirr as they dive for mosquitoes. But at Lac La Hache, at least the people in motorhomes were insulated from the sound of logging trucks.

And at Lac La Hache, we swam among goldeneye and not one of us came down with swimmer's itch, though the signs all warned against it. My daughter bought three Indian dolls at the overpriced store, two naked but for diapers and one in a fur robe with a green feather in her glossy hair. I tried to imagine the early days of that area and couldn't, no thread of witches' hair to go by, no mark in the gravel to guide me. But at night, after the logging trucks had passed on their fast journey south, I could hear loons and muse about camping, its curses and its blessings. My mother always said she hated it, but I remember her cheerfully stirring a pot of something on the stove, instant mashed potatoes maybe, and I remember there were marshmallows as a treat in the evenings. Sometimes we sang. Always we were stung by mosquitoes until we barely noticed them anymore. And when the sleeping bags came out to be aired before each new trip, I breathed in the odour of old campfires and all the places we'd pitched our tent, strands of memory deeply woven into the pattern of blue plaid.

Cool
Water

I SPENT AN HOUR or so this afternoon picking blackberries with my two younger children. Despite the heat, nearly ninety degrees, we wore heavy sweatshirts, long trousers, and high rubber boots to protect us against the brambles. We went to a favourite spot, not the trail to Ambrose Lake with its piles of seedy bear scat all around the berry bushes under the Hydro line, but to the end of Jervis Inlet Road, where two kinds of blackberry vines crowd the banks leading down to the sea.

I had mixed feelings about picking two kinds of blackberries. I'm not usually a purist about such matters, but I feel a certain loyalty to Himalayan blackberries, *Rubes discolor*, the kind I picked as a child on Matsqui prairie in the Fraser Valley. I remember my father pointed out a farm, the James Farm, and said that old James was responsible for bringing Himalayan blackberries to North America from Scotland in the last century. I don't know how true that is, and it does have an apocryphal ring, but I thought those blackberries the very essence of high summer. Although there were occasional pies (I don't remember jam), the way we usually had them was in yellow melmac bowls with a scant teaspoon of brown sugar strewn over and then milk. The milk turned pink and had the tiny fine hairs of the berries floating on top. We always planned to pick more than we did. The taste of berries and sugar and milk inspired us to plan all sorts of expeditions with buckets but somehow we got sidetracked and there were only ever a few desserts.

The other kind of berry we find is the evergreen bramble, *Rubes lacineatus*. The leaf is different, the berries ripen slightly later and are huge and full, larger than the Himalayans. I hate to admit it, because these berries fill a bucket faster than any others I've picked, but their flavour is disappointing. The smell of ripe blackberries doesn't rise from the depths of the plants, either, so I don't think it's only in my imagination that they aren't as heady as the others.

But we picked both kinds, hot in our heavy clothing and watchful for wasps. My son picked almost half an ice cream bucket full. My daughter, younger and impatient, found a small green caterpillar to play with and make a home for among dock leaves and plantain in her bucket, to sing to, and to plan a life for on the shelf in her room. Our dog ran up and down the road, barking at garter snakes which slid noiselessly down into the tangle of blackberries.

We talked about what we'd do with the berries. My son asked for a pie, my daughter wanted hers with yoghurt and honey, mixed and then frozen in the ice cream maker. I told them we'd have both these things and that if we picked enough I could make pancake syrup as well. While we picked and talked, the sun burned above us in our unseasonal clothing. There was complaining, of course, but I reminded my children that we had our bathing suits in the truck and could stop at Ruby Lake for a swim on the way home. They wanted to leave right away but I kept reaching down into the bushes for the ripe berries that my son had given up trying for, filling my bucket and then his. I didn't want to stop because I knew how pleased I would be, come January, to find the bags of blackberries at the bottom of the freezer, how good a pie would taste in the heart of winter, the fruit sweetened with vanilla sugar, maybe a few apples added, thick cream melting into the buttery pastry. Although I intend to come back for the unripe berries, maybe in a week, maybe two, who knows what will happen, I thought; this might be the last chance. So I told them to find something to do while I filled the last bucket, concentrating on the big evergreen brambles to make the picking go faster. My daughter sang a sad song for the caterpillar which had died from the heat of her hand.

When at last we filled all the containers we'd brought and it was too hot to even think about anything else, we changed into our bathing suits – no one lives at that end of the road – and piled our sweaty clothes on the floor of the truck.

At Ruby Lake, another family was just leaving our favourite swimming spot so we had the whole little beach area to ourselves. The children plunged right in, squealing as their bodies met the water. I was slower, standing knee-deep and splashing handfuls of water up over my shoulders, rubbing away the pink juice of blackberries from my wrists. Finally I pushed myself forward into the cool water of the lake, scattering a family of ducks, the two ducklings nearly grown and all that remained of the original seven. My children played in the lake they have known all their lives, the shore trees a little bigger each year, the same turtles basking on the logs left over from the days when the lake was a holding pond for logging on this part of the coast, the same arc of sun from east over the mountain to west over Agamemnon Channel beyond the lake. When I was a child, I ate blackberries in a yellow bowl, had a labrador who cooled her ankles in a lake, like this one does, lapping up water. We picked blackberries then, ancestors of the ones waiting in the truck, brought from Scotland to provide something known and loved for a man making a new life for himself in Canada.

Days of Gold
and Fireweed

WE'RE CAMPED BY WILLIAMS CREEK, warbling loons calling from a lake somewhere deep in the spruce woods beyond the road, coffee thick and dark to warm the hands against the chill of this mountain air. At the edge of our campsite are stunted pines and Indian paintbrush, and across the moose meadows, vast drifts of fireweed.

We came by road, the same road in places that they took then, hung by cantilevered beams above first the Fraser and then the Thompson River, north of the terrifying confluence of the two. Although I'd seen photographs for years of the Cariboo Wagon Road, it didn't occur to me that the tunnels I'd driven through many times on trips to the Chilcotin or farther north were relatively recent, some younger than I was. Those men heading north were balanced for their very lives high above the rapids or on wooden trestles along the canyon walls. Their ikons wander the road, still, heads resolutely forward, leading mules laden with supplies. Many fell to their death along with nervous mules and rough packs. One famous photograph shows a freight wagon and several men passing a huge beak of rock above the Thompson River north of Spences Bridge at Great Bluff. In the background are the hills of sage and bunch-

*An early Barkerville street
scene, circa 1865.*

grass, the same hills we passed coming on the newer road above the
unchanging river. 1865, telegraph wires already strung, the mules looking forlorn across the distance of years. I wonder if they're the same
mules in the photograph, same year, taken after a freight train arrived in
Barkerville. A few men in frock coats lean against a building and the dri-
vers have obviously headed straight for the saloon because the mules
stand untended. Slightly off-centre in the photograph, a child sits on a
log looking straight at the photographer. The child may or may not be
holding a cat in its arms. My own children drifted through the streets of
Barkerville more than a century later, one idly shooting a pop-gun of Victorian design, purchased in the Barkerville store, one with a cheek
bulging with jawbreakers, one looking so intensely at each building that

I knew he felt as I did, heard the voices just out of focus beyond the walls, the clatter of hooves as the freight came in.

What astonishes me in the early photographs of Williams Creek is the barren look of the mountains surrounding the townsite. Now they are cloaked in pungent spruce, aspen, pines, and the ground is thick with wildflowers – paintbrush, bunchberry, yarrow, lupin. I wonder how long it took before the land forgot the total assault of men upon its riches. Trees taken for houses, firewood, the lumber for the waterwheels used to pump the shafts dry. At a mining demonstration, a man told us that most of the lumber went into the cribbing used to support the mine shafts underground. Ten times as much lumber under the streets as on the surface. The creeks themselves were rerouted, wrestled from their courses, and everywhere the piles of tailings and the bare washed rock of the later hydraulic operations.

We came for an afternoon and have been here four days. Expecting a mecca for tourists thirsty for the authentic experience, we thought we'd just walk through, buy a postcard or two, and then leave. And yes, there are tourists walking the dusty main street, buying loaves of sourdough bread and having their pictures taken in period costume or else hidden by bubbles in the funny old bathtub. And we've done these things, too – well, not the session with the photographer but certainly we bought the bread, we walked the main street. In fact, we've walked it many times at every hour of the day, even late in the evening as security guards locked up and checked each area. We wanted to feel that sense of the streets at dusk when the light would have come from soft oil lamps and the smell of woodsmoke would have drifted from each chimney, the air ringing with the voices of miners changing shift, the saloons bursting with customers, hurdy-gurdy girls cajoling for drinks.

On a balcony above the street, a miner played a hammer dulcimer, the thin notes of an Appalachian lullaby drifting down over our heads and holding us in a net of memory. They came from everywhere and anywhere – Charles Blessing from Ohio, John "Cataline" Caux from the French Pyrenees, Billy Barker himself from the rivers of England, and nameless others. Or others, named but forgotten to us, lying under earth in the sloping graveyard, some with rough crosses, weathered as the men must've been before their time. Accidents in mine shafts, typhus, violence, and the dates on a few crosses attesting to death by old age. More men than women, several babies and children. Some stayed after the creeks ran emptied of gold and made lives for themselves, raised families, sent sons to both world wars. The graveyard, sheltered with trees, looks out over Williams Creek, the heavy equipment on its far bank undreamed of by those early miners.

Beyond the creek are the vast meadows of fireweed, brilliant acres of magenta. Would there have been fireweed then when the miners were taking down the trees, shovelling tailings onto the banks of the original creek? Or maybe it appeared later to shelter the wind-seeded trees growing up among the detritus, stabilizing the soil against the ravages of snow and spring runoff. How beautiful it would've looked to the women at Williams Creek, in summer, to see the spires of fireweed rising out of the bare slopes, to be gathered with blue lupin and scarlet paintbrush to fill jugs for the table. Behind some of the cabins are remnants of gardens – gnarled old lilacs and stands of delphinium – now overrun with nettles and cow parsnip. Some of the women must've brought seed with them, knowing that flowers would make almost anything bearable. Or else packets of precious flower seed travelled up the wagon road along with rubber boots, window glass, eggs, and pianos. Some women must've longed for roses, neat rows of pansies, tall hollyhocks to nod by the windows. I wonder about their days, when the children were at school in the little building by the church and their men were either mining for gold or weighing it at the assayer's office. Everything would have been difficult – heating water on woodstoves to fill the hip-baths that I saw for sale at the mercantile and the washing machine on the porch of the boarding house, keeping the floors clean when the front doors opened into parlours and nothing was paved. Did they often wonder where they'd been brought to and why? I think of Sophia Cameron, her untimely death by typhoid fever in 1862, still in mourning for her child who died en route to Williams Creek. Or Scotch Jeannie, dead in 1870 after her horse and buggy tumbled over one of the slippery treacherous banks. Some days it must've been heaven, clear air off the mountains and the new smell of sawn lumber.

At midday the smell of horse dung and dust is heady. We sit in front of the hotel and drink root beer, listening to the pleasant sound of water and voices. I give the children money to buy twists of brown paper full of candy from an elderly lady in a prim dress with a cameo at her throat. I want something for myself, too – not candy, though the saltwater taffy looks good, but something to transform my life upon occasion so that this is all a part of it. Maybe the tin candle lamp, a pattern of stars perforated in the reflector, or a bustle, or lace-edged knickers with a drawstring at the waist and a clever opening for relieving oneself. I buy a stick pen and elegant stationery and beeswax candles though it isn't what I meant. After hanging over the blacksmith's gate for what seems like hours, talking to the smithy as he pounds coarse metal into pothooks, my son is given a nail, made by the smithy that morning. After Barkerville burned to the ground in 1865, it was immediately rebuilt from the ashes and those ashes were searched for nails to use again, metal too precious to waste. Someone comes out of a building and begins to play a sqeezebox, someone else a fiddle, and soon a whole group of them are singing right in front of us. Oddly, it's a song my children have learned at school and they hum along, connected to the moment by a melody I've never heard before.

There is something very peaceful about the streets at twilight when the window glass catches the last sun and gives you back your own reflection. I want to sit on the little pink settle in the assayer's house, the room dimly lit by an oil lamp painted with roses, looking out to see whoever I might see. Word might come that someone has hit the motherlode and the streets will sing with whoops and cheers, maybe even gunshot by dawn. Later, when I'm lying in the tent with the sleeping body of my family all around me, I try to dream my way back into that house with the dark street on one side, the golden creek on the other. The loons warble and moan wistfully while a soft wind rises. I move in and out of sleep, disoriented by weather and the unfamiliar sounds of the night as near as the back of my hand. We could be a pack train heading north, the driver wanting to make Alexandria before stopping for the night, canvas bundles creaking in their ropes.

My son buys a goldpan to try his luck and his father drives him out the Bowron Lake road to find a stream. Although it's high summer, we have a campfire against blackflies; I sit with my coffee and maps, figuring out the old way here, the original way along Keithley Creek to Swift River and up to Richfield. The town of Antler, for instance. In 1861 there were over sixty houses and businesses, including a sawmill. There was a race-track, too, for horse races held each summer. I wonder what would be left. So much has changed, the trees grown up all around, trails abandoned, the roadhouses burned to the ground. Some memories must still contain images of those days, not firsthand of course in 1992, but maybe only a generation removed. There are stories somewhere, rounded and smooth as pebbles from the telling and retelling, handed down until finally a restless listener casts them away without a true idea of their worth. When we drove up the canyon, I couldn't pass the signs indicating the roadhouses without deep nostalgia, wordless and plain. On high ridges above the Fraser River, cattle grazed oblivious of what passed all those years ago. 100 Mile House, where there was "an ample supply of fresh beef, beans, cabbage, pies, milk, tea and coffee," Lightning Creek, and Cottonwood. In a photograph taken at Soda Creek in 1919, a tidy ranch nestles in a flank of the hills with some resting cattle, a few chickens, two cars to indicate comfort, and a line of immaculate laundry blowing in the wind. I suggested pulling off the highway at Soda Creek, somehow expecting this evocative image to present itself to us, unchanged, but found only a truck stop and a tired campsite without a single tent.

We eat our evening meal at Wake Up Jake's. Fussy table linen and odd Victorian landscapes locate us in time. We eat huge plates of roast pork with applesauce, chutney, root vegetables, wonderful rhubarb pie and thick sweet cream. Judge Begbie sits at an opposite table, a bottle of claret at hand and his hat and cloak on a bentwood rack beside him. He is talking to a young man about the finer points of a case involving claim jumping, and I want to lean to him, say "A hundred years from now I'll be playing on your grave in Ross Bay Cemetery, a child of seven, the same age as my daughter who, as you see, won't finish her dinner." A young woman in a long cotton dress comes out of the kitchen, wipes her hands on her apron, and sits at a harp. Closing her eyes, she plays "Star of the County Down" in such sad slow strains that I wipe a few stray tears from my own eyes. It is not only for the music I cry but for the ghosts who stand by her harp. Ned Stout, John Fraser, Madame Bendixon, coming in off the street to request, each in turn, a song, an air to keep them from passing out of memory. Outside the sun is falling behind Barkerville Mountain, the last rays gilding the fireweed with such golden flame that we are all touched by its heat.

Undressing
the Mountains

I HAD NOT REMEMBERED the mountains to be so visible. Driving to the Pacific rim, five days before Easter, I am shocked at the way they have been clearcut, shorn of their trees. This has been in the news, of course, and I've written letters to various politicians about forests I am familiar with at the age of thirty-nine – the Caren, the Carmanah which I knew in my days of canoeing the Nitinat triangle and hiking the West Coast Trail, the last of the spotted owl habitat around Lillooet Lake. But these mountains, high and austere above Kennedy Lake and Taylor River, are not what I think of when I hear about the Clayoquot protests, even though this stretch of Vancouver Island was once a place I came to as though to the arms of my family.

Who was I then, the woman who drove a small red truck through Sutton Pass in November, desperate to stand among the shore pines and bog laurel, and who walked the long beaches in 1973, naked but for delicate shells laced with seaweed to her throat and ankles? Now, I am arriving with my husband, our three children, and many suitcases. Our parents follow in separate cars, with similar luggage. We have reserved a duplex cabin one row removed from the beach, complete with bedding

back with my book in a Cape Cod chair, wishing I'd brought sunglasses. Our parents sit at the picnic table and talk about elderly neighbours with their eccentric habits, how much the campsite next door charges, what it charged five years ago, their arthritis, a friend's brain tumour, the price of bacon at Mr. Grocer. My husband cheerfully moves between the groups, agreeing or disputing so nicely that no one can tell the difference, while I am sullen and quiet, remembering how it used to be.

In so many ways nothing has changed, although in Tofino every second place advertises whale-watching trips and the shops are full of sweatshirts with the familiar grey whale tail arching over, in purple and teal green and raspberry pink. At Wickaninnish Beach, we see no one for hours and my children run in the breakers. They find sand dollars, crab shells, goose barnacles, and a headless sea lion carcass rotting in the sun. I show them eagles and a long tangle of bull kelp strewn with barnacles. Our parents sit on logs, happy in sunlight to watch their grandchildren write messages in the sand: *Have a nice journey!!* (to be read by migrating whales); and their names, to claim the day. Later there's coffee in the Wickaninnish Centre and a picnic lunch set out on some bleached logs, a few Steller's jays waiting for crusts. I want to walk the beach until the sand ends, maybe at the point of land curving to Vargas Island, but there's the whale-watching trip we planned a few weeks earlier, so we load up in the truck again and drive to Tofino where we are given red all-weather flotation suits and told to walk down the hill to the dock. "Look for the *Chinook Key*. Your skipper for this trip will be Carl." Carl takes us to see a nesting pair of eagles on a small island in the harbour and then we head out to sea to find whales. The sea is not choppy, but there are big swells and one of my children hangs over the side to vomit in the waves. My mother is sick. The whales do not appear as I dreamed they would, huge and near, but we see spray and a bit of back and a few shows of tails rising just out of the water. There are smooth lengths of water that we are told indicate whales beneath the surface. I ask if they travel in family groups and the skipper tells me yes, but there are also groups of two males with one female and he has seen them mating, one male supporting the female while the other copulates with her in the green water. I turn my head to hide tears.

Out on the water, I can see the mountains, clear against the eastern sky. Some of them are bare and scarred in the late March light, and this startles me, being accustomed to the sight of mountains draped with low cloud or else treed to their summits. At Sutton Pass, when we drove through a day or two earlier, an entire mountainside was denuded. There was so much waste. A creekbed running down the mountain was full of logs. No fringe of trees was left on its banks to shelter young fish, or to give shade to amphibians, or to protect the banks from falling in on themselves. In the letters I get back from the politicians I write to, I am told things are different now, rules are enforced, wildlife respected, habitat protected. And yet these mountains stand in the elements, unprotected and vulnerable. And they go on for miles in their shame.

The skipper takes a long way back to Tofino, around Vargas Island and Stubbs Island, hoping, I guess, for something dramatic to show us. Trees crowd close to rocky shores – cedars, hemlocks, Sitka spruce – and are draped with moss. A pair of loons swims close to the shore in one little bay and a small rocky island is dark with cormorants. "I bet that's called Cormorant Rock," I say to the skipper. "Well, Shag Rock, actually. They're always there," he replies. I had hoped to see the vast bodies of grey whales rising out of the water, but instead, there are birds, trees, and the naked mountains, one of them ringed at the peak with high white cloud.

In the evening, after a walk along Mackenzie Beach as far as we can go until we're stopped by the tide, my husband and I take our children to the swimming pool. We soak in the hot tub, telling ourselves that we'll sleep like babes tonight. Children shriek and splash in the blue pool and when it's time to leave, I find myself shy in the changeroom, trying to cover my body as I struggle out of my bathing suit and into my t-shirt and leggings. Two other women are changing, too, helping their children; they think nothing of standing naked to dry off a child. Twenty years ago, I walked on the beach wearing nothing but my necklace of shells, thinking only of the beauty of the waves. This night I am ashamed of my loose skin and heavy breasts, and I hold a green towel with pink palm trees under my arms as I pull on my underpants. When I see the two women later, out on the grass with the sweet stars above, I look away, embarrassed.

On our way home, we stop at Ucluelet so our parents can shop for trinkets and drink coffee in a converted ship, and we drive out to the coast guard station at Amphitrite Point. Each of us has a souvenir – shells, a little flag with a killer whale, and a memory of cormorants muttering on a stony island. Our suitcases are stacked in the back of the truck, our cameras and binoculars accounted for. Then we take the Port Alberni Highway east, towards home, thinking how much everything has changed and yet remains recognizable enough for nostalgia. When we drive past the first huge clearcut, crisscrossed with wasted timber, stumps charred and streambeds littered, I look up high to see waterfalls, silver chains shimmering down the necks of the mountains. Twenty years ago, the girl bedded down under stars, made her fire in a ring of stones, and tied back her hair with seaweed. She returned as a mother, heavy-fleshed and wrinkled, sharing with the mountains something of their great burden of shame and sadness, wishing for low cloud, at least, to give privacy.

Yellow
Plates

I FOUND THE YELLOW PLATES on the day before Thanksgiving, 1991. We'd gone by boat down the length of Sakinaw Lake, tying up to some logs at the western end. From there, a boggy path leads through wild mint and arums to a small estuary. High cliffs on either side of the bay give the place a protected hidden feeling; you could be at a creek mouth at the edge of the world.

We'd gone for oysters and clams for our Thanksgiving dinner. The tide was out but on its way in; thin October sun washed everything with chilly light and the stink of seaweed hung in the air. Three eagles sat impassively at the very tops of a couple of snags. They'd obviously been fishing – the salmon were rising and leaping in the bay, preparing for the swim up the creek into Sakinaw Lake, and to the gravelly mouths of two small tributaries coming down off the mountain. Every year we'd watch the salmon spawn, marvelling at the size of them – these were sockeye – and the tiny area where they'd lay their eggs and then die, their bodies washing in to the grassy shore and rotting in the fall air, eventually picked clean to the bone by scavengers. Further north, the Tsimshian had a song for this cycle:

I will sing the song of the sky.
This is the song of the tired –
the salmon panting as they swim up the swift
  current.
I walk around where the water runs into whirlpools.
They talk quickly, as if they are in a hurry.
The sky is turning over. They call me.

The earth turning on its axis, the year with each seasonal element – bud, leaf, fish, spine; this was what we witnessed on that still shore, just ourselves and the mirror of the sky.

John took a bucket and began to dig for clams on a sandy stretch, helped by a child or two. I took the other bucket and a knife to pry oysters from the undersides of the huge rocks on the opposite side of the bay. I was in shadow the whole time, reaching under and scraping my knuckles on the unseen colonies of barnacles as I felt for oysters. When I located one I'd find a place to brace my legs while I bent over to remove the oyster, sometimes loosening it with just my hands, sometimes sliding my knife under one edge of the shell and levering gently. Sometimes my hands touched a spiny mass of starfish as I reached under rocks. I imagined them waiting there, purple and ochre, mouths to the rock, feeding on mussels and barnacles, clusters of stars hidden in the shadows of the bay. The tide was steadily moving in and I wanted to finish while I could still return to my family by crossing the creek; when the tide was high, there was no easy way to get back and once or twice I'd had to make my way into the woods along the edge of the creek until I found a log to cross back on.

Wading across the rising creek, I suddenly spotted an unusually large shell on the bottom, partly obscured by eelgrass. Curious, I lifted it out and put it in my bucket among the frilly oysters; it rang against the side of the galvanized bucket like a bell. Not a shell, then, but what? By now the tide was surging in and I made my way over the rocks to the place where the rest of my family had finished filling their bucket with butter clams and littlenecks. We sat at the high-tide line, drinking hot chocolate from a thermos and watching the eagles, who, accustomed to us by now, had begun to leave their snag, one of them swooping low over the bay and rising with an arching silvery fish in its talons. It disappeared around the cliffs and the other two followed. A few pleasure boats drifted by and in the distance was a troller returning to Pender Harbour, too far away for us to read the name.

Remembering my strange disc, I took it out of the bucket and showed the others. Holding it up to the light, turning it this way and that, we could tell that it was a plate but so covered in mud and algae and even a little group of barnacles fastened to the rim, that we couldn't tell what colour it was. I scraped away a corner of the algae with my oyster knife and was startled to see brilliant yellow showing through. The weight of the plate suggested pottery or ironstone rather than lighter bone china. How long had it been at the bottom of the creek, a small sun eclipsed by eelgrass, how many sockeye runs had passed over while it lost its light under the tides and seasons? By then there was almost no beach left and the wind was blowing northwesterly and cold off Agamemnon Channel so we left to walk back along the trail to our boat.

To our right as we walked, there was an abandoned fish-counting shack between us and the creek. Tucked down in the trees and sided with roughcut shakes, it looked almost like part of the underbrush. We'd seen it many times but had never really explored it. This time, for some reason, I wanted to peer through the small window to see what was inside. There was broken glass around the door and old tins and a midden of shells. Half in, half out, an iron bedframe leaned against the door and the floor had rotted through, sword ferns growing into the room in one place, shattered window glass and bottles all over. A rough shelf hung partly off one wall and on the shelf were four dusty yellow plates, the only things in the shack that were unbroken. They were waiting, as the first plate waited, in a dark corner, not underwater, but fallen the same, five suns from a flying heaven. I took them, not wanting them broken when the shelf fell from the wall, or buried when the roof fell in as it threatened to do as I left the shack behind. It began to drizzle so we hurried to our boat, tossing on its length of rope.

We were with the wind going back. The small boat flew up the lake as if winged and our eyes were sharpened by wind. Here and there a fish jumped in joy under the bowl of watery sky where the stars were hidden in their colonies, and trees moved in and out of the mist like quiet animals. The summer cabins were closed for the year, windows shuttered against winter weather. Years ago, this lake was a long arm of the sea. Fishermen from the early years of Pender Harbour remember coming up the arm in their herring skiffs, out of storms. They fished sockeye in what is now the bay and probably paused in their skiffs to look at the pictographs on the tall cliff, some now submerged after the damming of the narrow entrance into the arm sometime in the late 1940s, done to control water levels for the sockeye run. The pictographs are red ochre, some fading with the years, but most of the images are still visible. Fish, certainly, prawns, and even what looks like a crayfish, something we'd found in the creek on different occasions; long sticks that might be fishspears or harpoons; a canoe shape and two images that look like ladders and might be weirs. It would make sense if the coastal Indians had constructed a fence weir across the entrance, dip-netting or gaffing the salmon as they collected against the lattice. At a small bay in Pender Harbour, remnants of stone traps can still be seen at low tide and middens of clam and oyster shells testify to the repeated use of the area as a fishing site. As with every other time we came by boat down the lake, we paused at the pictographs, let them speak their own mysterious poetry about the place, the history, the rich bounty of the sea.

By the time we reached the little launching spit at the eastern end of the lake, it was almost dark, light falling in the west over Nelson Island beyond Agamemnon Channel and the blackness edging down to the lake from Mount Hallowell behind us. We drew up the boat onto its trailer, placed our buckets carefully in the back of the truck, the oysters blanketed with seaweed, the clams opening and closing in the cold water.

Thanksgiving, 1991. We ate the oysters broiled in their own juices with lemon over top, clams stewed with garlic and garden tomatoes, turkey and all the classical trimmings, served on the yellow plates. We each said a grace before eating, something to be thankful for – food, family, the peace of the big trees around us and the weather bringing rain, wind, the brilliance of sunlight in October, sometimes streaming from the great sun above and sometimes hidden in creekbeds, shacks, flawed under dust and barnacles, waiting to be found and praised.

Carol Ships

for Edith Iglauer Daly

EVERY YEAR WE WATCH the carol ships from our friend's sundeck overlooking Garden Bay. These are not the large decorated pleasure boats that make such a beautiful procession in Burrard Inlet and English Bay each Christmas – I've seen those too – but a small fleet of fishing boats, dinghies, working and charter boats that carry carollers around the perimeter of Pender Harbour.

Our friend invites people to come for dessert. We all bring a favourite thing –fruitcake, mince tarts, brownies, strudels – and these are placed on a long pine table. My children, dressed warmly, are pink-cheeked with excitement as we say our greetings and find a place to watch from on the crowded deck. The boats leave the government wharf in Madeira Park at seven and then make their way slowly to Garden Bay, winding in and out of the little bays and around the points, pausing now and then as watchers on the shore sing out to them or else signal a message with a flashlight. It's difficult to hear the music though one or two boats have loudspeakers. The night is always cold and what you hear is a phrase or two of song carrying across the water, chilly and sweet under the stars. *Join the triumph of the skies …* We begin one song, *O come, all ye faithful*, and then stop for a moment as we realize we can hear the refrain of "We Three Kings" riding the current in to where we stand. *Westward leading, still proceeding, guide us to thy perfect light.* It's gone before we know it. The boats have lights strung along rails, up masts and throughout the rigging so that they look like floating Christmas trees crossing the harbour. Some boats have coloured lights outlining life preservers. The carollers may carry lamps or flashlights which move and twinkle in their distance. *Long lay the world in sin and error pining …* We sing, of course we sing, whatever song comes to mind and no one is self-conscious in the dark. My children love "The Huron Carol" and we are usually the only ones who know more than one verse so we sing of the hunters and the babe wrapped in rabbit skins and the humble lodge, and I think I've never believed more in the nativity than at those moments, singing with them in the cold night. *This holy child of earth and heaven is born today for you.* The boats move slowly, like winter constellations, and we watch until they disappear.

Inside, the oil stove warms the kitchen and our friend is busy with coffee and hot chocolate. Coats go into the guest room with its twin beds and ancient quilts; eventually a child may find her way in there and fall asleep on the pile of parkas and heavy sweaters and will awake at midnight to discover herself being moved gently aside in the search for a jacket. When the child is my own small daughter, I am reminded of waking among the fur coats – what would they have been, muskrat? – as a child myself, and coming out to the party, wondering if I'd dreamed the music, the carols of a family Christmas. Some people gather in the kitchen to discuss boats and politics, two topics of perennial interest in our community. Others carry plates of dessert and cups of strong coffee into the living room where a window seat looks over the dark harbour and a fire snaps and blazes. The carol sheets from the local newspaper have been saved and brought to the evening, and in this room we sing too, not in darkness and mystery as we sang to the boats, but in a more deliberate harmony. Children who would not dream of singing out loud at school or elsewhere ring out like high-voiced birds, unbroken sopranos carrying carol after carol. Sometimes my oldest son brings a recorder and accompanies us as we sing "Good King Wenceslaus," and "Hark the Herald Angels Sing," and when we've finished, the true notes of the final chorus hang in the air for a moment or two. The older people are quiet, perhaps remembering other Christmases, other rooms with familiar people, the same carols.

This year I wondered if the children were too old and thought we might be too busy with Christmas visitors to come to see the carol ships. But when the evening arrived, I cut slices of fruitcake to put on a platter with sprigs of holly, we bundled up the visitor in scarf and mittens, and when the ships came around the point, we were there, singing on the sundeck. Later, in the warm living room, my friend directed carols, having had the piano newly tuned. Parts were delegated and my husband was given Melchior to sing, my oldest son, Balthazar. My husband's mother sat beside him on the couch, not having heard him sing since childhood, touched by his low clear voice. I sat with my daughter and younger son, singing the familiar chorus: *Star of wonder, star of night, star with royal beauty bright.* Outside the stars shone over us like they shone over the three Magi on that cold plain nearly two thousand years earlier, familiar as the carols that keep us together on these nights in the middle of winter. *Alleluia, the earth replies.*

ACKNOWLEDGMENTS

VERSIONS OF INDIVIDUAL ESSAYS in this collection have been published in *Geist*, *Matrix* and the *Vancouver Sun*. "Cool Water" was broadcast on CBC's *Crosswords*. "Undressing the Mountains" will appear in the anthology *Writing the Land*, edited by Pamela Banting.

Specific thanks: to my family (John, Forrest, Brendan and Angelica Pass) for being such good companions; to Charles Lillard for providing maps, books, clippings, references in letters and talk to suggest directions; to good friends for everything from smoked fish to information on tides to advice on campsites; to Terry Glavin for editorial skill and inspiring conversations; to Carolyn Stewart and Audrey McClellan for careful attention to detail; and to Rolf Maurer for publishing my book as part of a great series.

The Tsimshian song on page 88 is from Franz Boas' *Tsimshian Mythology*. I am indebted to several sources for photographs: Kelly Nolin at the British Columbia Archives and Records Service; the Ashcroft Museum; my parents Shirley and Anthony Kishkan; and my son Forrest Pass, who suggested the photograph of Harold Pass at his workbench to accompany "The Tool Box."

The dedication at the beginning of this book doesn't nearly tell the story of my gratitude to Gayle Stelter for her steady encouragement, friendship, support and generosity over the years. She is missed beyond words.

PHOTO CREDITS

Page 32: British Columbia Archives and Records Service No. E-03456; p. 45: BCARS A-00350; p. 48: BCARS D-03171; p. 55: Ashcroft Museum; p. 76: BCARS C-08171.

Copyright © 1996 by Theresa Kishkan

Published by New Star Books Ltd. All rights reserved. No part of this work may be reproduced or used in any form or by any means – graphic, electronic, or mechanical – without prior permission. Any request for photocopying or other reprographic copying must be sent in writing to the Canadian Copyright Licensing Agency (CANCOPY), 900 - 6 Adelaide Street East, Toronto, Ontario M5C 1H6

Please direct submissions and editorial enquiries to: Transmontanus, Box C-25, Fernhill Road, Mayne Island, B.C. V0N 2J0. All other correspondence, including sales and distribution enquiries, should be directed to New Star Books, 2504 York Avenue, Vancouver, B.C. V6K 1E3

Transmontanus is edited by Terry Glavin
Series design by Val Speidel
Cover photography by Gary Fiegehen
Map courtesy Clear-View Maps Ltd.
Production by Rolf Maurer and James Lewis
Printed and bound in Canada by Best Book Manufacturers
1 2 3 4 5   00 99 98 97 96

Production of this book is made possible by grants from the Canada Council and the Cultural Services Branch, Province of British Columbia

CATALOGUING IN PUBLICATION DATA
Kishkan, Theresa, 1955-
Red Laredo boots

(Transmontanus, ISSN 1200-3336; 6)
ISBN 0-921586-49-3
1. British Columbia – Description and travel. I. Title. II. Series.
PS8571.I75R42 1996   C814'.54   C96-910636-x
PR9199.3.K444R42 1996